BRAY – DID YOU KNOW...?

ABOUT BRAY – DID YOU KNOW...?

In June of 2011, I posted an old photograph of Bray to a friend in America using the social networking website Facebook. I was amazed when I visited my friend's page a few days later to see that the photo had received so many 'likes', shares and comments – and all of them positive.

It was then that I realised that creating our own Facebook page for old photos and stories of Bray would be a good idea, and would probably attract a few hundred people to join it. So, in July, my brother Stephen and I had the new 'Bray – Did You Know...?' page up and running.

Over 2,350 people have now joined our Facebook page, and more are joining daily, but over the past year or so we have encountered many people who didn't have a Facebook account, or even access to the internet, and thus were unable to enjoy our posts and stories on Bray – Did You Know...?, So, there was only one thing for it – to turn all those stories and photographs into a book.

This book, which contains stories that have never been posted on our Facebook page, is aimed at providing factual and entertaining information on the history of our town of Bray here in County Wicklow. The stories are about Bray's history, people, buildings, monuments, statistics, businesses, schools, amenities etc. Whether you are a current or former resident of Bray, or fondly remember visits there, this book is a must for you.

There have been quite a few excellent books published about Bray and its history, but we feel that this book is unique, as most of the stories – whether a single page or several – are unusual and diverse, plus they all include one or several historical photos.

We have thoroughly enjoyed researching and putting together the pages for our online page and, indeed, this book. We have lost count of the many hours we have spent in the various libraries and newspaper archives collecting information – but looking at this book now...I sincerely think it was all worth it.

So I hope you enjoy our Bray – Did You Know...? book as much as we enjoyed producing it.

Brian Lennon
Bray, County Wicklow
November 2012

For Billy, June and Monica

BRAY – DID YOU KNOW...?

A fascinating, true and sometimes strange collection of facts about Bray, County Wicklow, in stories and pictures.

Brian Lennon & Stephen Lennon

The Liffey Press

Published by
The Liffey Press Ltd
Raheny Shopping Centre, Second Floor
Raheny, Dublin 5, Ireland
www.theliffeypress.com

A catalogue record of this book is
available from the British Library.

ISBN 978-1-908308-36-8

Printed in Spain by GraphyCems.

CONTENTS

CONTENTS

The bandstand on Bray's esplanade was made by the famous Hammond Lane Foundry Company Ltd. who operated from their large premises at the Dublin Docks for many years. But did you know that on the base of several of the bandstand's supporting columns the word DUBLIN is actually misspelt? It should state: 'HAMMOND LANE FDY CO LTD DUBLIN' but in fact, as you can see (right) it states: 'HAMMOND LANE FDY CO LTD DUBILN'.

BRAY - DID YOU KNOW...?

County Wicklow · Ireland

braydidyouknow@gmail.com

The Bandstands
(Part I of III)

When a tourist visits our town of Bray there is no doubt that amongst landmarks like Bray Head, the esplanade, the promenade and the town itself the bandstand in the centre of our esplanade will surely stay in their memories. Most of us have memories of the bandstand, whether it was as a youngster running and jumping on its large wooden floor or watching a performance by musicians or an entertainer. But did you ever wonder where our bandstand came from? In fact, did you know we had three bandstands on our esplanade at one stage?

Long before these bandstands were erected on our seafront, there already was a small bandstand on the esplanade. It had a long flag pole in the centre, it was also low to the ground, had no roof and was very plain.

When the Irish International Exhibition at Herbert Park, Ballsbridge, Dublin finally closed on November 9th 1907, the process of dismantling the buildings and the disposal of the materials in six auctions began. Because of their size, most of the buildings were dismantled and the materials sold off. Smaller buildings such as pavilions, kiosks and machinery sheds were dismantled and re-erected on new sites.

Above centre: The entrance to the International Exhibition at Ballsbridge. Right: A photo of Bray seafront c. 1898 showing the old original bandstand in the background.

© Bray - Did You Know 2012

4

The Bandstands (Part II of III)

Three bandstands were purchased by Mr. McDonnell, Town Clerk of Bray Urban District Council. Minutes from May 6th 1908 state: *"Bray Urban District Council agrees to purchase from International Exhibition grounds the bandstand [Main bandstand] and re-erect it ... fear of too great a size".*

On July 18th 1908, the minutes state that the *"new Bray bandstand formally opened before 4,000 people; 11th Hussars, Scotch and Lancashire Fusiliers Bands; several Dublin vocalists also engaged."*

The three bandstands were purchased from the Exhibition to be placed on the Bray esplanade. One of the smaller bandstands was placed opposite the railway crossing (at Quinsborough Road junction)...

to be continued...

Photo courtesy Barbera Flynn

Clockwise from above right: A postcard from the 1907 International Exhibition showing the Bray bandstand during the show; A close up of the bandstand shortly after being erected at Bray; The new Bray bandstand in all its glory (minus clock) c. 1910; Some small changes have occurred with the bandstand, but this is it today.

The Bandstands *(Part III of III)*

...another was placed where the present bandstand is now and the third opposite Lacy's Hotel (The Esplanade Hotel). The Northern bandstand opposite to the railway crossing was known as the 'Day Bandstand', but is long gone. The existing bandstand was called the 'Evening Bandstand' and the small bandstand at Lacy's was reserved for visiting variety shows. Many entertainers played the bandstands over the years and during the annual Bray Regatta there was always entertainment on the bandstands. Entertainers included, not only musicians, but also comedians, ventriloquists and dancers etc. The White Coons, Drury's Argyle Minstrels and Val Doonican appeared on the bandstands. In 1946 Ted Young rented the Evening or small bandstand and presented a variety show entitled 'Bray Breezes' featuring Jack Gregory, pianist, Alf D'Alroy, magician and 'Babette and Dorena', The Dinty Dancing Darlings.

Even in modern times some big names appeared on the main bandstand, including Paddy Casey, Sinead O'Connor (who lives nearby), Brian Kennedy, Mary Black, Lisa Hannigan, Bagatelle, U2 tribute band *Rattle & Hum* and the popular 1970s band *Stepaside*, made their video 'The Last Resort' on the bandstand.

There is no doubt that our bandstand is an icon of Bray, and hopefully the people of Bray will enjoy, not only its character, but the entertainment it brings for many generations to come.

Clockwise from top: A photo c.1909 from Royal Marine Terrace, showing the Northern Bandstand, which was known as the 'Day' bandstand; a close view of the 'Small' Bandstand, opposite the Esplanade Hotel, venue for countless variety shows until it was demolished in 1960 because the roof was dangerous; the small bandstand during the 1950s (note the bad state of the roofing).

BRAY-DID YOU KNOW...?

Raheenacluaig Part 1: This name translates in English to 'The Little Raith of the Bell' (as a matter of interest there is a bell on display in the Hunt Museum, Limerick, called the 'Bray Bell." A Bell appears on the Bray Coat of Arms.
Twenty eight paces south east there was a piece of ground enclosed by a trench. It was said that this was a cemetery for children who died unbaptised.

A few centuries ago, a rough road led from the church through the grounds of Presentation College. Much later on in 1780 a pedestal of a cross with ancient markings was found. The cross belonging to it is supposed to be buried in the hedgerows to this day.
The bulldozers working on the old Pitch and putt facility are said to have scattered the bones of the little children to many obscure and unconsecrated holes by the church. To be continued...

BRAY-DID YOU KNOW...?

Raheenacluaig Part 2: This poem was written to the memory of the Lost Children of raheenacluaig:

Beneath Bray's towering craggy head, Rest the windswept ruined hallowed stones,

That once sheltered the tiny bones, of innocent babes long, long dead.

Interred in ancient holy ground, without the sound of a funeral bell,

No hymns, priests prayers or mourneful knell, But the caoining and cry of seabird sound.

On grassy slope with aspect fair, Sanctified and blessed by mothers tears,

Their nightmares realised, awful fears..confirmed, nothing now but deep despair.

Angel souls not to heaven bound, But into Limbo, so we were told,

By teachers in foolish days of old, These unbaptised babies were to be found.

For them no funeral mass was said, Just a plot of ground in some penal day, Beside that little rath in Bray.

No mark or record where they were laid, in earth forgotten and yet blessed, where once eagle, falcon

and raven fly, Singing a sad lament, no lullaby.

Their tiny corpses uncaressed,

Raheennacluaig, lonely and forlorn, no history, no memory now recalls,

what once occured outside it's walls....Babies all unnamed, no one to mourn.......

BRAY • NOW AND THEN

County Wicklow · Ireland

braydidyouknow@gmail.com

After the new Quinsborough Road was built from the Main Street to the seafront and railway station in 1854, the new junction at Main Street and Quinsborough Road was to become known as the *'hiring corner'*. Groups of men, and sometimes boys, would congregate here in the hope of being hired for a day's work somewhere in or around the Bray area.

The two gentlemen standing outside Leverett & Frye's (right) now Finnbee's Juice Bar – certainly look like they are of working class and waiting at the *hiring corner*.

Let's hope they got a few days' work somewhere!

The Knight, the Virgin and the Devil

In 1875, Ravenswell (later to become the home to the Sisters of Charity) was purchased by Lord Meath for his son and heir, Lord Brabazon, who was returning home after spending much of his life abroad. The last owner, Mr. Matthew O'Reilly Dease, had previously allowed the local people access to Ravenswell Road – as at the time it was the only access to the seashore north of the river mouth – however Lord Brabazon told the Bray Commissioners that he was 'restoring the estate' and ending the practice of letting it become a 'common place of convenience' and put up gates to halt access to the seashore. This enraged the people and resulted in nearly a year passing involving court hearings and legal debates as to the right of way for locals, but eventually the people of Bray won their right to access and right of way was again granted.

But Brabazon lost more than an argument – the conflict isolated him from the townspeople and created many enemies. Soon after he decided to build a Town Hall as he thought this would enhance his own image in the town and ease ill-feeling among the people.

The monumental fountain outside the Town Hall, locally dubbed 'The Devil' was originally designed as a base for a statue of a knight in armour representing a Meath antecedent. But in 1882, during the period of popular ill-feeling against Lord Brabazon, his architect Sir Thomas Newenham Deane suggested that this statue of the knight should be replaced by a statue of The Virgin 'who traditionally presided over fountains to ensure respect for the work of art. *"I do not know whether you would think this was pandering to the Roman Catholics... we have as much right to the Virgin as they have"*. There is no recorded response but subsequently the design incorporating the Wyvern, a Meath or Brabazon family heraldic design, was adopted.

In 1885 another dispute arose, it represented the final participation of Kilruddery in the municipal affairs of Bray after a period of 275 years.

Left: Lord Brabazon; Right: An impression of what the monument at the Town Hall could have looked like; Inset: The wyvern was eventually chosen by Lord Brabazon over the Knight and the Virgin.

BRAS - DID YOU KNOW...?

County Wicklow · Ireland

braydidyouknow@gmail.com

St Cronan's School *(Part I of IV)*

In many ways the history of a school can be the history of a town and none more so than St. Cronan's Boys National School. The present school was opened on the Vevay Road (or Convent Hill as it's called locally) on 19 September 1932, but its origins date back as far as 1820 when on July 20th of that year a school for boys and girls was opened on the Seapoint Road, which was to play an important role in the development of education for Bray's poor Catholic population.

The school was a single storey building which still stands today, it is in no way easily recognizable as a schoolhouse, having been converted into dwelling houses around the turn of the 19th century. It was, in fact, two schools, one for boys and one for girls. The latter closed in January 1901, the establishment and growth of Loreto and Ravenswell schools having made it redundant.

But the school was reported to have been in a 'dilapidated state' by the 1860s, and with the growth of the town, lack of space was becoming a problem. The answer came finally in 1880 when a new school building was built at the rear of the Church of the Most Holy Redeemer on Main Street – it is now the Little Flower Hall.

to be continued...

Bray Boys National School c. 1900. This photo was taken at the side of the Holy Redeemer Church.

Top right: The Register of Religious Instruction for 1893; Above centre: The old school building on the Seapoint Road; Below right: The school behind the Church is now the Little Flower Hall .

BRAY - DID YOU KNOW...?

County Wicklow · Ireland

braydidyouknow@gmail.com

St Cronan's School *(Part II of IV)*

However, by the end of the 1920s the same problem would occur at this school, now Bray Boys National School. Some classes were held in Brighton Terrace (now Parnell Road) due to overcrowding. Another move, the second, was inevitable, this time it would be to a much larger and modern premises on the Vevay Road, this would be St. Cronan's National School.

The new school was built at a cost of £11,000, involving a debt of £3,863. A book was opened for contributions, the Archbishop gave £500 and other large contributions amounted to £900. There were many well known principals at St Cronan's, including the first headmaster Mr. Patrick McDonnell, who had come up from the school behind the church. After Mr. McDonnell, who was one of the last of the old gentlemanly type of schoolmasters (he was known affectionately as 'Paddy Mac' by his pupils), came Mr. Martin Daly, whose nickname was 'Nigger' Daly. He was succeeded by Michael Nolan. Mr. Jim French became headmaster in the 1940s and remained until Mr. Seán Cotter took over in 1975. From the Teachers Return No 1 of January 1963, we see that Mr. French began teaching at St Cronan's in 1931 at the age of 21 after training in Drumcondra.

Other teachers over the years included: Mr. 'Cockey' Ward, Mr. Clarke, Mr. Sean Donegan, Mr. McMahon and more recently Mr. Lewis, Mr. Lavin, Mrs. McGinn, Mr. Russell, Mr. Davis, Mrs. Murphy, Mr. Barry and Mr. Vaughan Dodd (Principal).

In the 1947 Roll Books, notes to Mr. French from parents give a picture of the poorer families in Bray in the post-war years. Many pupils were kept at home because their only pair of shoes were leaking, others had to work or do messages, and in January 1948 due to flooding on the Dargle Road. There were also several requests for help in obtaining schoolbooks due to poor family circumstances.

to be continued...

Scoil Cronan Naomhtha, Bray, C o. Wicklow—The pupils "ringed" will each receive 10/6 on applying to the Secretary, Independent Newspapers, Ltd., enclosing an identification voucher signed by the Principal (Mr. Patrick MacDonald).—Irish Independent Photo. (H.).

Top right: St Cronan's on the Vevay Road; Above left: Pupils just after moving to the new St Cronan's school; Above right: Mr. Daly, Mr. Ward and Mr. Clarke in 1932.

St Cronan's School *(Part III of IV)*

In June 1954 a circular was sent to managers and teachers of national schools about special arrangements for school children to help at the harvesting in view of the difficulty in saving the crops...owing to the exceptionally bad weather conditions. Pupils aged 10 and over were permitted to absent themselves for not more than 10 school days in the period up to 17 December 1954 to help on the land of their parents or guardians.

But one cannot write about St. Cronan's without referring to its most famous past pupil, Cearbhall Ó Dálaigh, who was enrolled in the school from 15 April 1918 to 8 May 1920. Born on 12 February 1911 upstairs at 85 Main Street, Bray (now Jasmine House restaurant), Cearbhall was the second son of fish and poultry manager, Richard Daly. In 1915 he was enrolled at the Loreto Convent but the mother superior asked his mother to withdraw him after one day. He then went to St Cronan's and the family moved to 3 Old Court Terrace, Vevay Road. They left Bray when Cearbhall was aged 13 after the death of his father. He attributed his love of the Irish language to the influence of teachers: Mr McDonnell, Mr Honan and Martin Daly (father of John Daly).

Cearbhall Ó Dálaigh became Chief Justice in 1961 and in 1974 was inaugurated as the 5th President of Ireland. Mr Ó Dálaigh died in March 1978 at the age of 67. He is buried in Sneem, Co Kerry.

to be continued...

Above: McCabe's shop, Cearhhall Ó Dálaigh was born upstairs; Top left: Cearbhall Ó Dálaigh who was a student at St. Cronan's; Top right: A section of a 1948 school roll book; Bottom right: (L-R) Morgan Walsh M.A., James French M.A., & Heber Mahon M.A. at U.C.D. October 1941 (note the sand bags in the background).

BRAY - DID YOU KNOW...?

County Wicklow · Ireland

braydidyouknow@gmail.com

St Cronan's School *(Part IV of IV)*

After nearly seventy years at the old St. Cronan's school building, it was time for another move and again to a larger premises. Construction of a new school building on grounds once belonging to Loreto Convent started in 1998 and on November 2 1999, the teachers and pupils moved into the new building, which boasts 15 classrooms, 4 resource rooms, and a state of the art computer room. The official opening of the school took place on June 18, 2001. Soon after, Gaelscoil Uí Chéadaigh took up residence in the old St. Cronan's school building. In 2008 St Cronan's received funding from the Department of Education to build a new extension, which included 3 additional classrooms and 3 resource rooms. The new building would replace the unsightly prefabs adjacent to the school. The building work started on the 5th of January 2009 and was completed in August 2009.

Yes, St. Cronan's Boys National School has certainly come a long way since its humble beginnings on Seapoint Road. It has seen Bray grow from a population of 2,000 to over 26,000. Many of the ideals which parents cherished over the decades are being realised today. Paddy Mac must be smiling in heaven to see the school under its new principal, preparing the boys to be young Europeans as they learn French, Spanish and German. Clearly the school's greatest influence was through its past pupils, those thousands of decent Bray men in all walks of life. One would hesitate to pick out any one of them for special mention, but like Cearbhall Ó Dalaigh, all were surely proud of their association with Bray's oldest educational tradition, St. Cronan's.

Clockwise from left; The new St. Cronan's from the air (before the extension) 2009; The new rear extension; The entrance to the new school; Inside one of the old classrooms of the old original school; The old St. Cronan's school.

© Bray - Did You Know 2012

14

The Lagoon at Bray Seafront

Walking along the very stony beach north of Bray harbour, you can't help but notice the old rubbish including broken bottles, tin cans, old bicycle frames and car tyres etc. protruding from within the dangerous and continually eroding cliffs. This is due to the fact that the Bray Urban District Council (BUDC) had used this area behind the north beach - or back beach as the local call it - as a landfill dump for many years.

Although the dump was under the jurisdiction of the BUDC the beach was the responsibility of Dublin County Council from whom it received scant attention. Consequently, it was a kind of 'No Man's Land'.

It is hard to believe that there was once a beautiful lagoon here, or that as time went on, the town dump was allowed to expand northwards towards the lagoon. This picturesque wildlife habitat was home to a variety of wild animals and birds, and it was a place one could visit and experience the peace and tranquility.

But in the early 1960s, the BUDC made another infamous decision to use this wonderful lagoon as a continuation of the landfill dump, and alas it was no more, destroyed forever for the many generations that would never see Bray's beautiful lagoon.-

Black & white photos: Four different views of the Lagoon on the Back Strand, or north beach during the late 1940s and 1950s.
Bottom left: A recent photo of the area where the lagoon used to be, now part of the old landfill.
Bottom right: A photo taken on top of the landfill site.

BRAY – DID YOU KNOW...?

County Wicklow · Ireland

braydidyouknow@gmail.com

The 'Crossing Sweepers' of Bray

Roads in Bray in Victorian times were un-tarred and made of earth and rough stones that with any bad weather rapidly turned to mud. Constant horse and cart traffic mixed manure with the mud, which resulted in the edges and hems of Victorian dresses being soiled and splashed by the wheels of the horse drawn vehicles throughout the town.

To combat the problem large granite slabs with borders of smaller granite pieces were placed at crossing points between footpaths for people to walk on. It was the usual practice for a man or boy, called a 'Crossing Sweeper' to stand at these crossings so that when a member of the gentry would approach, he would sweep the pathway of mud and manure in the hope of a reward of a farthing or two for his services.

The last two surviving granite crossways are at the top of Florence Road at the junction with Main Street and at the junction of Duncairn Terrace and Seymour Road.

Right: A 'crossing Sweeper' looks for his reward after sweeping the crossway. Far right: The crossway at the top of Florence Road.

© Bray – Did You Know 2012

16

BRAY – DID YOU KNOW...?

County Wicklow • Ireland

braydidyouknow@gmail.com

BRAY
DID YOU KNOW?

THE MIRACLE

MADE IN BRAY

ARDMORE STUDIOS IRELAND

KING ARTHUR

THE MIRACLE

FROM THE DIRECTOR OF 'MONA LISA'
A film by NEIL JORDAN
BEVERLY D'ANGELO • DONAL McCANN

THE MOST ENCHANTING COMING-OF-AGE COMEDY-DRAMA SINCE WHATEVER WERE HERE'

FANTASTIC, WITTY, CLEVER IT'S A WONDERFUL FILM

Directed and written by Neil Jordan, this 1991 movie stars Beverly D'Angelo, Donal McCann and Niall Byrne. 'The Miracle' tells the story about two teenagers Jimmy and Rose who spend their holiday in Bray. Out of boredom they observe other people and imagine wild stories about them. One day they observe the blonde Renee, and Jimmy is immediately fascinated by her and even follows her home. She, too, seems to like him, but for a mysterious reason keeps him at a distance.

KING ARTHUR

RULE YOUR DESTINY JULY 7

Made in 2004, 'King Arthur' stars Clive Owen, Stephen Dillane and Keira Knightley.

DID YOU KNOW...

• Although the weather seems very cold and dreary, the movie was shot during near-record high temperatures in Ireland.

• The camera operator wore a motorcycle crash helmet and was constantly surrounded by men with riot shields because of the intense action sequences happening around him.

THE SWASTIKA LAUNDRY

The Swastika Laundry Company was founded in 1912, their head office was on the Shelbourne Road, Ballsbridge, Dublin, and branches situated at No.9 Main Street, Bray and in Dun Laoghaire. The Swastika Laundry was founded by John W. Brittain (1872 – 1937) from Manorhamilton, Co. Leitrim, who was also the proud owner of a famous horse of the time called 'Swastika Rose,' a horse that was well known to those who frequented the RDS Show in Ballsbridge.

The laundry used electric vans that were painted red with a black swastika on a white background to collect and deliver the laundered goods to their customers. The company ceased to exsist in the late 1960s when it was bought over by the Spring Grove Laundry Company who occupied the same building in Ballsbridge. From the late 1960s to the early 1980s the laundry chimney was emblazoned with a large white swastika which could be seen from many distant places in the surrounding areas.

Top left: The old Swastika Laundry shop in Dun Laoghaire; Top right: A religious procession passes by the 'Bells & Swastika' Cleaners c. 1947 (which later became 'Sasha' Boutique and ' Euro Savers'; Bottom: Some of the vans that the company used to deliver their goods.

BRAY – DID YOU KNOW...?

BLAST FROM THE PAST

BRAY
Photos by John Hinde F.R.P.S.

A well known John Hinde postcard of Bray from the 1960s. Bray was a top seaside resort back then and tourists poured in in their thousands from all over the UK and Ireland to visit our town. The arrival of the package holiday and affordable family cars were partly to blame for the demise of the resort.

braydidyouknow@gmail.com

BRAY DID YOU KNOW?

© Bray - Did You Know 2012

The Seaside Resort

The Esplanade, Lawns and Head, Bray, Co. Wicklow.   Colour Photo by John Hinde, F.R.P.S.

A popular Hinde postcard of Bray's Seaside Resort from c. 1960.

Dr. Kinahan and his new Bray species

Dr. John Robert Kinahan was born in Dublin in 1828, and was the brother of G. H. Kinahan of the Irish Geological Survey. He obtained the M.D. degree at Dublin University, lectured under the Science and Art Department on botany and zoology.

He was Secretary of the Natural History Society of Dublin. He wrote extensively, largely on local botany, geology and zoology, being especially interested in native ferns; and was a leading figure in Dublin scientific life.

In a lettter to a national newspaper, Dr Kinahan described a strikingly distinct species of *Crangon* as the *Crangon Allmanni, Kinahan,* or *Channel-tailed Shrimp*: "Carapace smooth, excepting a small spine on the median line of the gastric region, and one on each branchial; second pair of legs as long as third; sixth segment of abdomen deeply channeled above; channel continued as a shallow groove on terminal segment; third joint of anterior pair of legs spined; a minute spine between the insertion of second pair of legs in males; in the female, spine obsolete. Length from one inch and a half to three inches. It is of bluish-grey colour, dotted over with brown, red and gold."

The species was found by Dr. Kinahan in the coralline zone of the Irish Sea, near Bray, County Wicklow in December 1856, and also in February 1857.

Dr. Kinahan has described as *Pagurus Eblanensis* what he himself subsequently thinks may be the *P. ulidianus*; and under the name of *Porcellana priocheles*, what is perhaps "merely a young form of *P. longicornis.*" He has kindly forwarded to us the brief description of what he deems a new species of *Hippolyte*, found along with the *Crangon* at Bray and at Dalkey.

Hippolyte Andrewsii, Kinahan. Allied to *H. Cranchii.*

"Apex of rostrum with three teeth above; median plate of tail furnished with five pairs of lateral spines; external antennae longer than body; second pair of legs five-jointed. Colour is rose-pink, with darker bands; ova bright emerald-green."

Dr. Kinahan wrote a few works about Zoea larvae *[Liljeborgia kinahani (Bate, 1862)]* and wrote extensively on Irish Cambrian trace fossils. He died in February 1863 at the age of only thirty-five years.

BRAY – DID YOU KNOW...?

County Wicklow · Ireland

CATASTROPHE AT THE BRANDY HOLE VIADUCT *(Part I of II)*

The railway line which cuts through the mountains between Bray Head and Greystones was designed by Isambard Kingdom Brunel and was praised as a wonderful engineering project. Brunel was an English civil engineer who built bridges and dockyards including the construction of the first major British railway, the Great Western Railway; a series of steamships, including the first propeller-driven transatlantic steamship; and numerous important bridges and tunnels. His designs revolutionised public transport and modern engineering. Though Brunel's projects were not always successful, they often contained innovative solutions to long-standing engineering problems. But Mr. Brunel's railway design at Bray Head soon became known as 'Brunel's Folly' due to the expense of maintaining it that had been incurred over the years through accidents and rock-falls etc.

On Friday, 9 August, 1867, a major accident occurred when a passenger train traveling north from Wexford on route to Dublin crashed at the viaduct entering the Brabazon Tunnel at Bray Head. A sudden subsidence of the line caused the locomotive to derail and plunge into the sea below. The fireman was killed immediately, and an elderly passenger died some days later in hospital, but remarkably the rest of the passengers weren't seriously injured, as the carriages remained upright.

■ *Isambard Brunel, the designer of the railway line at Bray Head.*

■ *An image of the aftermath of the crash on the Brandy Hole viaduct which was used for a newspaper at the time.*

to be continued...

21

CATASTROPHE AT THE BRANDY HOLE VIADUCT *(Part II of II)*

Luckily the engine derailed to the land side of the bridge it's thought that if it had derailed on the sea side of the bridge it would have pulled most of the passenger carriages with it into the sea, which could have ended with catastrophic consequences.

The earliest help to reach the scene of the accident were brought by boats from Greystones (a few miles south of Bray), the fishermen having seen from the pier that something was wrong. The injured were transported by goods wagons out the Harcourt Street line (which ceased operating in the 1950s) which forked off and ran through Shankill to a point near Loughlinstown at St. Columcille's Hospital, from where they were carried across the fields to get treatment.

The subsidence necessitated the building of a new tunnel next to the existing tunnel, which opened in 1876. The site of the accident, near the abandoned tunnel, can be still seen from parts of the Cliff Walk and from train as they approach / leave the new tunnel.

■ *Clockwise from top right: The new tunnel under construction c. 1874; A close up of the new tunnel (left) and the old disused tunnel; A DART passes the site; The crash made main headlines in London.*

BRAY - DID YOU KNOW...?

County Wicklow · Ireland

braydidyouknow@gmail.com

The Stones of St Paul's *Part I of II*

Some interesting entries in the list of burials in St. Paul's Churchyard...

• Ellen (Nellie) Neville, Bray Commons. Age 96. Buried December 20 1877. Was maid of the Inn at Woodenbridge in the rebellion of 1798.

• Marie De Beaux, a teacher at the French School (Sidmonton Place). Age 27. Buried August 1, 1879.

• Burials from the Cripples' Home :-
Eliza Martin. Age 20. Buried June 11, 1879; Jessie Williams. Age 14. Buried Aug. 27, 1879; Henry Carter. Age 9. Buried Feb. 25, 1880; James Parsons. Age 10. Buried June 14, 1881; Margie Cameron. Age 7. Buried Aug. 5, 1881; Henry John Keegan. Age 15. Buried Oct. 7, 1882; William Williams. Age 7. Buried June 3, 1883; Lucy Floyd. Age 19. Buried Nov. 20, 1883; Catherine Adams. Age 12. Buried May 8, 1884; Susan Florence Whitton. Age 8. Buried Nov. 26, 1884; William Alcock. Age 6. Buried May 23, 1885; James Bryan. Age 14. Buried July 16, 1885; James Wilson. Age 11. Buried Sep. 10, 1886; Mary Franklin. Age 9. Buried March 18, 1887;

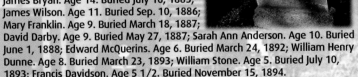

David Darby. Age 9. Buried May 27, 1887; Sarah Ann Anderson. Age 10. Buried June 1, 1888; Edward McQuerins. Age 6. Buried March 24, 1892; William Henry Dunne. Age 8. Buried March 23, 1893; William Stone. Age 5. Buried July 10, 1893; Francis Davidson. Age 5 1/2. Buried November 15, 1894.

The Cripples' Home was founded in 1874 by Lucinda Sullivan for receiving and training crippled children from all parts of the country. It was located on the Lower Dargle Road and was the foundation for the Sunbeam House institution.

• Lucy ("Lucinda" in register) McKay, died November 4, 1833. Age 32.

• Christopher Thompson M.D., F.R.C.S.I., 9 Duncairn Terrace. Age 62. Buried December 19, 1876. The obelisk outside the Royal Hotel is dedicated to Dr. Thompson who had treated many Bray people with the cholera virus – he later died from the disease himself.

• James McKay died November 5, 1833. Age 41. (*It is said that Mr McKay's body was stolen the night after the funeral by body snatchers. A heavy sarcophagus now covers the grave, with names on top and a latin inscription on the east end).*
James McKay was the schoolmaster & Parish Clerk in Bray.

• Elizabeth Fox, (mother of blind Ben Polard's wife, Upper Commons Road). Aged 75. Buried January 17, 1887.

• John Hughes, Purcell's Fields. Age 9. Buried March 6, 1867. Was a nurse child, attended Bridge School, and after his death the children collected money to erect a small cross, which stands against the wall at the head of the grave.

• John Nixon Read Esq., 69th Regiment, Bray Strand. Age 72. Buried December 5, 1864.

• David Smith, native of Gothenberg, Steward of the ship 'Leonia', wrecked at Bray. Age about 23. Buried October 3, l876. Also, James Mariner Ackles, of Nova Scotia, Mate of the same ship. Age 23. Buried, October 19, 1876.

• Mary Mahon. Loughlinstown Workhouse, aged 50. Buried November 21, 1873.

Above left: Cripples Home burial plot;
Above right: Dr Christopher Thompson's grave.

to be continued...

BRAY - DID YOU KNOW...?

County Wicklow · Ireland

braydidyouknow@gmail.com

The Stones of St Paul's *Part II of II*

• **Large Enclosure:** The Burial place of the Edwards Family, Old Court.
The first entry under this name in the register is: David, son of Richard Edwards Esq. Buried July 9, 1668. The last entry under this name in the register is: Emily Edwards, 2 Clarinda Park E., Kingstown. Age 95. Buried April 11, 1885.

• **Old stone inscribed:** *"HERE BODY *SAWI DO 1727"*
However, no burials are recorded in the registers between 1725 & 1728.

• **Commander A.W. Forbes R.N.** (Lieutenant Commanding Coastguard at this [Bray] station in 1858). Died at 11 Peter Place, Dublin, Age 71. Buried December 29, 1864.

• It is said that somewhere close to the tower entrance (left) were buried together:
Eliza Fox, Commons. Age 69. January 9, 1846.
William, her infant grandson. Age 2. January 13, 1846. There are no grave markings visible.

• **Henry Walker.** 2nd Battalion Coldstream Guards, died in his counrty's service at Bloemfontein, April 4, 1900.

• **The Putland family**
(1) Charles Putland, Bray Head House. Age 60. Buried October 6, 1874.
Also his wife:- (2) Georgina Putland, Bray Head. Age 62. Buried March 18, 1882. Also her sister:- (3) Frederica York Anderson, Bray Head. Age 55. Buried January 9, 1882. (4) George Putland, son of (1), Bray Head. Age 35. Buried October 16, 1876. (5) Charlotte Mab Neligan, eldest daughter of (1) and wife of John W. Neligan, Bray Head House & Tavistock, Devon. Buried October 10, 1887.
It was well known that Charles Putland and his wife were very kind and sympathetic to their employees and, indeed, to the poor people of Bray – especially during the famine years. They once lived at Sans Souci (Loreto Convent) before selling it to the nun's order, they then moved to 'Bray Head House' which eventually became home to the Christian Brothers at the present Presentation College on the Putland Road (which was constructed as a famine relief scheme by Charles Putland in 1863).

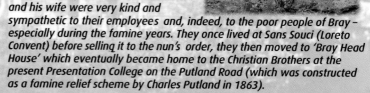

• **Lieutenant James Tandy** (for several years Chief officer of the coastguard on this station [Bray]). Died on the 22nd of January 1835, aged 45 years.

• **Moved from under site of new chancel:** stone with inscription:
This stone is erected here by Lettice Saunders in memory of her daughter Mary Saunders who departed this life the 3rd day of April 1807 aged 13 years.
The grass is green the rose is red,
Here lies my name now I am dead.
Mary Saunders.

BRAY - DID YOU KNOW...?

County Wicklow · Ireland

braydidyouknow@gmail.com

POSTCARDS FROM BRAY

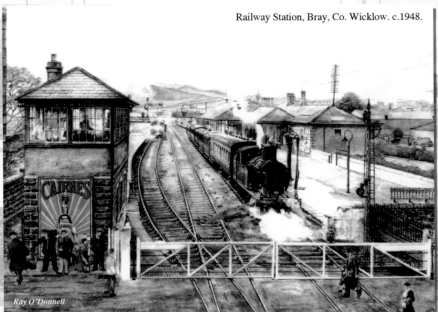

Railway Station, Bray, Co. Wicklow. c.1948.

Ray O'Donnell

One of three postcards of Bray Railway Station painted by Ray O'Donnell.

25

Was Bell's first telephone call to Bray?

Transcription of a tape recorded message sent in 1962 to Aravon School, Meath Road, Bray, by Fred Eason on the occasion of the School's Centenary.

"I went to the school in 1875, so that I am now in my 98th year. One of the most interesting things which occurred during my stay at Aravon was in 1876 when our headmaster, John Holdbrook, received from Professor Bell, the inventor of the telephone, with whom he had established a warm friendship, a pair of receivers for the telephone, which he set up between the main building and the outer classroom block; so that it appears that some of us Aravon boys were the very first ever to speak through the telephone."

Top right: Aravon School back in yesteryear;
Right: Alexander Graham Bell demonstating his new telephone device;
Far right: Bell's telephone protoype 1876.

BRAY – DID YOU KNOW...?

County Wicklow · Ireland

braydidyouknow@gmail.com

Breslin's Royal Marine Hotel *(Part I of II)*

On a prime spot right next to the railway station, Edward Breslin opened his hotel *Breslin's Bray Hotel* on 30th May 1855. The hotel had the advantage of wonderful uninterrupted sea views, but like all the hotels that would be built along the sea front, it had the disadvantages of a rather congested site and undue proximity to noisy steam trains. Soon after completion, the hotel was renamed *Breslin's Royal Marine Hotel*, and the new west wing was built over the gardens in 1860, which added an additional twenty bed and four extra sitting rooms; the hotel could now boast ninety bed rooms and twelve sitting rooms. The hotel was of fine design, as G.R. Powell states in his 1860 book *'The Official Railway Handbook to Bray, Kingstown, The Coast & The County Of Wicklow'*,

"Entering the hotel by a portico and flight of steps, we find ourselves in a tastefully-arranged corridor, terminating in the large room already mentioned as opening into the grounds. On our left is the coffee-room, a luxurious apartment, commanding a magnificent view northward along the four mile strand to Killiney, and eastward, the level sweep of the esplanade and the sea beyond. The private sitting-rooms upstairs open on balconies commanding, on every side, extensive views of sea and mountain – the western windows especially opening on a beautiful prospect. Mr. Breslin is indefatigable in his exertions to ensure the comfort of his visitors".

Son of a 'small farmer' from Baltinglass in Co. Wicklow, Breslin had worked his way up from house steward to become a successful hotelier and businessman in the town of Bray.

to be continued...

Bottom left: A fine photo of the front of the hotel; Top left: The ladies drawing room; Top right: The hotel with Bray Head in the background c. 1880; Right centre: An early drawing of Breslin's Bray Hotel (before the west wing was added in 1860; Bottom right: The rear of the hotel and garden c. 1880.

Breslin's Royal Marine Hotel (*Part II of II*)

Breslin's Hotel stayed in one ownership until Breslin's death. But the valuation was reduced in 1877 from £300 to £150. By 1910 the hotel had been purchased by the Bethall family and renamed the *Marine Station Hotel*, the Bethall's also owned the *International Hotel* over the railway and the *Bray Head Hotel* at the southern end of the promenade.

But on 22nd August 1916 – after sixty years in operation – the *Marine Station Hotel* had its upper floors destroyed in an accidental fire and for twenty years the surviving fabric remained vacant, detracting immensely from the approach to the esplanade over the level crossing – a fact that the late Mr. Edward Breslin himself would not have been too happy about.

The building – at the junction of Strand Road and the Quinsborough Road – was eventually purchased by the Great Southern Railway and was turned into a station buffet for many years, eventually its partial replacement by an undistinguished office block did little to enhance the site. The *Dug Inn* pub was on the site for many years, now *Katie Gallagher's* Pub is here and the adjoining apartments stand on the site today...a far cry from the once beautiful *Breslin's Bray Hotel* which opened its doors in 1855.

Clockwise from above: One of Mrs. Breslin's family tea parties on the terrace of the hotel c. 1885;
Guests of the hotel enjoy the sunshine and sea air on the terrace c. 1890;
A fine shot of people relaxing on the seafront and the Marine Station Hotel in the background;
Two of the original floors were demolished before the building became the GSR Station Buffet;
The site as it is today.

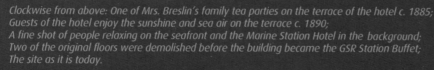

In its heyday, Bray Harbour was a very busy place with all kinds of vessels loading and unloading coal, sand, timber, grain and other cargo. Pictured below is a brig unloading in an unfinished Bray harbour c. 1893.

Coal here is being bagged in the hold, carried up on deck and slid down a chute to a horse and cart. Note the steam crane working on the newly built north pier in the background, the steam crane ran on a set of rails, and parts of the rail were still visible on the 910ft long pier up until a few years ago.

Lewis Bennett – The Seneca Chief

A member of the Snipe Clan of the Seneca Indians, Lewis Bennett showed extraordinary capacities as a long-distance runner in his youth. In fact, on the Cattaraugus Reservation in New York State, where he perfected his skills under his nation's traditional system of physical training, his speed and endurance gave rise to the legend that a horse had died of exhaustion after being outpaced by him for some thirty or forty miles.

By the mid-1850s, Bennett was running professionally, and in 1861 he went to England to compete with the best runners in the British Isles. He lost his first contest there, but was soon winning on a regular basis and finding himself lionized in sporting circles. In the spring of 1863, his times for ten-to twelve-mile runs set new records that lasted well into the 20th century. This photograph (right) was taken in England at the height of Bennett's fame there. As the picture indicates, Bennett revelled in reminding his English fans of his Indian origins, and he ran his races clad in wolf skin and a feathered headband. He is buried in Forest Lawn Cemetery, Buffalo, New York next to the grave of the Seneca orator Red Jacket.

An Indian Chief in Purcell's Field

A series of sports, under the management of Mr. Cassidy, came off in this locality on Saturday. They were held in Mr. Purcell's large field, and attended by upwards of 500 persons. The principal event of the day was a trial of speed in four miles by 'Deerfoot', the Seneca Chief, against Jackson, Mower, Andrews and Brighton, and after an exciting race of 22 minutes, was cleverly won by the Indian runner.

His running was much admired, and exhibited a vast amount of endurance – the pace at which Mower went was astonishing, but the son of the prairie outstripped them all. The sports concluded with sack-racing, ball-gathering, pole leaping, and other ancient sports. Musgrave in a running leap cleared ten feet nine inches. A programme on a larger scale will come off tomorrow in Mr. Crosthwaite's large field, Sallynoggin Road, Kingstown.

Freeman's Journal, 8th September 1862.

(Note: Purcell's Field is now St. Kevin's Square and James Connolly Square off Main Street, Bray.)

DEERFOOT,
THE SENECA INDIAN RUNNER.

Above: Lewis Bennett during one of his many races in Britain and Ireland;
Inset above: Bennett's headstone in Buffalo, New York, U.S.A.

The Seagulls (Part I of II)

Above: The 1953 / 1954 Bray Wanderers team.

The Bray Wanderers saga began in 1922 when a dispute in St Kevin's G.A.A. team led to some members leaving the G.A.A. and forming a soccer team, this became known as Bray Wanderers. Wanderers first home ground was on the Convent Hill/Vevay Road opposite Loreto Convent, then they moved to the G.A.A. grounds in Novara Avenue followed by Doyle's Field where Ledwidge Crescent (Palermo) is now. But the 'Seagulls' have long since settled at the Carlisle Grounds, near the railway station at Bray.

The Carlisle Grounds can claim to be the FAI League ground with the longest history as a sports venue. Opened in 1862 as the Bray Athletic Ground, it was renamed the Carlisle Cricket and Archery Ground later that year, in honour of the 7th Earl of Carlisle who performed the opening ceremony in his capacity as Lord Lieutenant of Ireland. The name was popularly abbreviated to The Carlisle Grounds as early as 1870.

Wanderers were runners up in the Sunday Alliance Div. 3 in 1922/23 and also Runners Up in the Sunday Alliance Division 1 in 1927/28. The town of Bray had three of the best Junior clubs in the country during the late 1920s, namely Bray Wanderers, Glenview and Shamrock Boys. Unfortunately Wanderers went into decline in the mid 1930s, but were reformed in the early 1940s. The present Bray Wanderers continues on the team founded by a group of young men in the early 1940s after the demise of Bray Unknowns.

Bray Unknowns had played a few seasons at the Carlisle Grounds around 1910. The club re-formed after the First World War and joined the League of Ireland in 1924, playing on the outskirts of Bray. In 1929 they moved back to the Carlisle and carried out substantial changes to the ground in preparation for their return. Unknowns built the main perimeter wall at Quinnsboro' Road as well as the terracing and roof over the 'stand' (usually called 'the Shed'). They re-laid the playing pitch and railed it off. It's an over-used expression, but they must have appeared such a progressive club at that time.

The pitch was subsequently re-laid on several occasions. For example, when Transport brought League of Ireland football back to the ground, many CIE staff from Bray and Dublin volunteered to work on the pitch. It's said that the excellent pitch drainage derives from the use of railway cinders as a base for the pitch at that time!

Above: The Bray Unknowns 1922/1923.

© Bray – Did You Know 2012

The Seagulls (Part II of II)

Above: The 1940 Bray Wanderers team.

The first League of Ireland match at the ground in the 1929/30 Season was a 2-2 draw between Unknowns and Dundalk. Fred Rogers opened the scoring for Unknowns, William Murray and John Aitken scored for Dundalk, and Johnny Payne equalised. Unknowns lined out: Dunne, Daly, Ebbs, Kane, Mainey, Fennell, Lally, Hogan, Rogers, Payne, Blackford. The referee was a Mr Nicholson, from Wrexham. A big crowd attended. In the longer term, financial problems appeared, and the club folded in 1944.

The Unknowns had been a springboard for some talented local players (Byrne was an early Republic of Ireland International while playing for Unknowns, and Farrell went on to better things with Shamrock Rovers), and brilliant goalkeepers (including some from across the water, such as Leckie).

The success Wanderers achieved was outstanding including the much sought after Bradmola Cup, Intermediate Cup in 1955/56 and again in 1957/58 and in 1958/59 they won the Leinster Senior League. This tremendous career culminated in the winning the FAI Senior Cup in 1990. Currently Bray Wanderers are in the League of Ireland Premier Division and are managed by Pat Devlin *(far right)*.

Bray Wanderers re-built and strengthened parts of the wall of the grounds in 1997-99 as part of the overall plan to improve access and safety in the ground *(below right)*. They installed new turnstiles on Quinsborough Road at the seafront corner and blocked up the old turnstiles along the same wall.

The new (1999) seating on the railway side of the ground is but a part of this work, and in December 2000 planning permission was granted for further development which will see new team and club facilities installed behind and under that stand. The installation of excellent modern floodlighting means that games can be played at any time and are not restricted to daylight hours. Early in 2001, Bray Urban District Council granted a 35-year lease in the Grounds to Bray Wanderers A.F.C., conditional on the use of the grounds being restricted to sporting activities.

From its history, the quirks and remnants of bygone days, the Carlisle can rank with Dalymount Park and Tolka Park in terms of special character, even if it can't claim the same prominence in football history.

© Bray – Did You Know 2012

Murder Mystery...on Bray Head *(Part I of II)*

Around about the year 1825, there was a farmily named Byrne living at the western slope of the Head. Old Byrne, who in his younger days was a fisherman and now was a successful farmer, his wife, two sons and daughter, Moya, all lived happily together. Moya was pretty and was "just verging from the blushing laughing-eyed girl into the more matured charms of womanhood". On visiting Bray's Main Street from time to time, while going on errands, she became friendly with a young man named Garret O'Toole, whose father and mother had died of the 'fever' when he was a child. A relative kindly took on the position of foster parent and taught him about farming as well as providing him with a good education. Garret, as he grew older, felt that he was a burden to his kind kinsman and eagerly sought employment so that he might become independent.

One day, while walking on the strand aimlessly throwing stones into the water, he was approached by a sailor who asked him if he would like a job. It was obvious to Garret that the stranger was an 'old salt' from the way he was attired. Garret readily agreed to perform whatever task was asked of him and he was immediately employed unloading a cargo of contraband from a vessel anchored off Bray Head. He was well rewarded for his services and from then on he was regularly employed in the activity of smuggling.

The friendship between Moya and Garret grew stronger until Moya decided that it was time that her father and mother were informed of their attachment to one another. She asked her mother to broach the subject with her father. When her father heard of the matter he ranted and raved and wouldn't give his consent to the friendship of the two young people developing any further. According to him Garret was nothing but a common smuggler without any hope of leading a successful life; the young man would end up at the end of a rope. His wife pleaded Garret's cause but without any success. Moya, being a dutiful and obedient daughter, promised her father that she would not introduce the subject again and that she would refrain from having any meetings with Garret.

On hearing this bad news Garret resolved to change his employment so that he might continue his friendship with Moya and be accepted with favour by her father. He had a substantial sum of money saved and with it he purchased some land, in Little Bray beside the Dargle, which he commenced to farm. Soon he was earning as much as he had been making from smuggling and it was inevitable that he was to meet Moya, by chance, Bray being such a small place. When they both renewed their friendship the young couple agreed that the time was ripe for another attempt to obtain the goodwill and the blessing of Moya's father.

A few evenings later the young man presented himself at his intended's home where he explained his changed and successful way of life to her father. Instead of being received with kindness and civility, poor O'Toole was chastised and ridiculed and the mother and father of a row ensued. He was ordered to leave the house, never to darken its door again, and angry words were exchanged aloud between them both...

BRAY – DID YOU KNOW...?

County Wicklow · Ireland

braydidyouknow@gmail.com

Murder Mystery...on Bray Head *(Part II of II)*

Subsequently, the same night, the old man went out for a breath of fresh air to cool his temper and perhaps to ponder on what had transpired. Had he acted too hastily? Was his decision a wrong one? Was he breaking his daughter's heart? These thoughts were running through his troubled mind as he went towards the cliffwalk that goes around Bray Head. That was the last time he was seen alive. When he failed to return to his home that night his family set out to search for him without success. The following morning, when the dawn had brightened up the day, his broken body was found lying above the high water mark beneath the cliff.

Foul play was immediately suspected and Garret was apprehended and committed to gaol where his trial was set for the following month at the assizes at Wicklow. All the evidence was against him, Moya and her mother were called to testify and under cross-examination they tearfully described what had transpired on that fateful evening. The row, the angry words, the heated arguments between both. Neighbours who were within hearing distance on that night were also examined and they, too, bore witness to what was said. Both Moya and her mother also told the judge that they believed that Garret could never have committed such a crime. But all the evidence was against him and the jury quickly returned a verdict of guilty. The judge was in the process of delivering the awful sentence of death when there was a commotion at the entrance of the court. Silence was ordered without any effect and into the body of the chamber came several fierce looking seamen, one of whom stated that he was spokesman for the group.

It transpired from the leader's evidence that they were all Arklow fishermen and that they were off Bray Head on the fateful night in question. They described the evening being a bright moonlit one and while they were hauling their nets they saw Mr. Byrne, whom they knew quite well, on the cliff path. He appeared to be agitated so they shouted at him to mind his step as he was seen stumbling a little but he didn't seem to heed them. They debated among themselves as to whether they should send one of their members ashore to give him assistance but on looking again they saw that he had recovered his equilibrium. There was no other person near him and they lost sight of him and assumed that he was safe. They now believed that he had again tripped and fallen over the precipice. It was only lately that they had heard of the trial and had rushed to the court to give evidence in order to save the life of an innocent man. The judge asked that all the seamen be sworn in and each testified to the truth of their leader's statement. Garret was immediately pronounced not guilty and the resounding cheers of all present signified their unanimous approval.

Garret and Moya, after a respectable period of mourning, resumed their friendship and were eventually married in Holy Redeemer Church and they lived happy long lives together. It is more than likely that the sailors, who came to Garret's defence in the court, were engaged in the trade of smuggling as Arklow fishermen would rarely, if ever, be fishing at night so near in to Bray Head and especially so close that they could recognise someone walking on the path. But whether Old Byrne was brutally murdered or simply lost his footing and fell to his death that night was never solved and shall remain a mystery for evermore.

© Bray – Did You Know 2012

BRAY – DID YOU KNOW...?

BLAST FROM THE PAST

Originally owned by the Putland family, Bray Head House was put up for Auction in 1912, it was not sold and subsequently lay vacant until 1917 when it was purchased in July 1917 by the Frame family for £8,000. It was then sold on in 1921 to the Presentation Brothers who started a school here. The house, now adjoining part of the old school, is today derelict and seems to be unused.

braydidyouknow@gmail.com

© Bray - Did You Know 2012

Bray Head House

Once Bray Head House - Presentation College c. 1920.

BRAY – DID YOU KNOW...?

County Wicklow · Ireland

braydidyouknow@gmail.com

The Bolivar and the Kish Bank

The early months of the year 1947 were to prove to be very severe for many of the population of Ireland. A food shortage still existed in the country due to the war and rationing of food, fuel and clothing was in force. It was against this background that the M.V.BOLIVAR was making her way across the Irish Sea on the morning of Tuesday, March 4th, bound for Dublin Port with a badly needed cargo of grain and other items. Like many another fine ship before her, the BOLIVAR would never reach the port and would leave her bones in the sands of that treacherous graveyard of ships that spans the entrance to Dublin Bay waiting to ensnare the unwary, the Kish Bank.

The BOLIVAR was almost new, at 137 meteres long, she was a steel-hulled vessel of 5230 tons, owned by the Norwegian shipping company of Fred Olsen and Company, a firm that still exists today. When the war ended, the fitting out of the BOLIVAR was completed and she set out on her first voyage. From Norway she headed for Santa Cruz in the Canary Islands, then she sailed to Buenos Aires in Argentina to discharge her cargo. She took on 5,000 tons of grain for Dublin and Liverpool, some bales of leather and a consignment of fruit, in addition to various other cargo items. The first port of call was Vigo in Northern Spain and from there she sailed to Liverpool where she arrived at the end of February. She next sailed for Dublin on the late evening of 3rd March; Captain Sigurd Rasmussen and the crew of the BOLIVAR would have had no inkling of the fate that awaited their fine new ship.

Radar had not yet become universally available to merchant shipping and it would seem that due to the limited visibility and the sea conditions that were now very rough, that the Kish lightship was not sighted and at 12.30am the BOLIVAR drove across the shallow sands of the Kish Bank and stuck fast.

The crew tried to manoeuvre the vessel off the bank, but to no avail. The wind direction and the falling tide both contrived to keep the ship stuck fast. As the tide dropped further the ship broke in two, and the fore part of the vessel swung clear and grounded about a hundred yards away from the stern section. Dun Laoghaire lifeboat station were made aware of the situation and when they got to the stricken vessel they rescued crew and passengers and all returned safe.

The beaches from Bray to Howth soon became littered with debris and flotsam from the wreck which was eagerly picked over by swarms of people despite the efforts of the Gardaí. Among the cargo were many bales of leather, and there are many stories extant about handbags and coats being made from these. The maximum depth of the seabed around this wreck is about eight to ten metres and on a calm day, with a low tide when anchored over the wreck, if you peer down you can see some of the growth encrusted wreckage just a few feet below the surface.

Top: The M.V. Bolivar taking on cargo; Centre: the ship in two on the Kish Bank; Bottom: The bow section of the Bolivar, photo taken from the salvage vessel.

© Bray – Did You Know 2012

36

BRAY – DID YOU KNOW...?

County Wicklow · Ireland

braydidyouknow@gmail.com

Little Bray Castle (Part I of II)

Castle Street is a very short street that runs northwards from Bray Bridge to join the Dublin Road near Ravenswell. The street got its name from the castle that once sat on the west side of Castle Street called Little Bray Castle. Back in 1459 when the castle was built – not long after the Battle of Bloody Bank – Little Bray looked a lot different than it does today. The castle, which was built with a grant of £10,seems to have been built in a miserably weak position next to the ford. We know it was once owned by the Archbolds, and is thought to have been built directly over the ford to defend the route from marauders from the south. The river was more of a ford at the time, was very wide at this area and ran through where Castle Street shopping centre and the old Bray Golf Club are now.

The Archbolds also held among them the manors and castles of Much / Great Bree, Killruddery and Raheenaclig (on the side of Bray Head). But by the middle of the 17th Century, the building was in ruins, so Cromwell had no reason to knock it to pieces – although the castle was later repaired. It was then described in Fleetwood's Survey as "one castle wall, the old castle valued by the jury at £5." In the same survey the castles of Ballyman and Old Connaught were valued at £20.

Local legend has it that supplies were transported by rowing boat, unloaded offshore and then hauled through a channel across what is now the fairways of Bray Golf Club. This was at a time when there was no harbour, nor was the river contained by walls. This was a busy place when the search was on for Michael Dwyer in the 1798 period.

to be continued...

Right: A 1932 photo of Castle Street with Little Bray Castle in the background. The building on the right is now Everest Cycles;
Middle: John Taylor's 1816 map showing the castle (ringed);
Far right: Little Bray Castle as it was c. 1918.

37

BRAY – DID YOU KNOW...?

County Wicklow · Ireland

braydidyouknow@gmail.com

Little Bray Castle (Part II of II)

The castle is long gone, but an extract from 'The Stones Of Bray' by George Digby Scott reads: *"The brick battlements on top are, of course, quite modern; but the walls beneath them, with the projecting dripstone ledge and the loophole in the southeast angle, and the small square window in the west wall, are probably ancient enough. The small carved head that projects from the east wall near the loophole (probably a portrait) is a peculiar feature of one of these very undecorated Irish castles, but has a parallel with Bullock Castle."*

The late Colbert Martin, who was a Bray historian, also wrote about the castle in a journal of the Old Bray Society: *"The castle appears quite deserted. The door in the street is somewhat old looking, and studded with big-headed nails. The buildings surrounding and leaning against this old tower, are*

chiefly modern, I should say, though an attempt has been made to give them a castellated appearance so clearly of recent time as possibly to divert attention from really ancient tower."

From 1837 the castle in Little Bray was used as a barracks for the constabulary and petty sessions were held there every alternate Saturday until the Courthouse at the Royal Hotel was built in 1841. The Earl of Meath, as lord of the Manor of Kindlestown, held court here through his seneschal every month. Later Mr Gerity, a butcher rented the castle, which was then sold into private ownership in 1905 but was unoccupied soon after as during the 1913 strikes, a relief centre was set up in the castle to distribute food and clothes to the needy. The Castle stood where the car park of the Castle Shopping Centre is now – opposite Heitons Hardware (now vacant). Unfortunately, the Castle was demolished in 1937 by the Bray Urban Council as part of a road-widening scheme. By that time the building had deteriorated to a dilapidated state

through neglect. The method of demolition used was a hawser looped through the windows and attached to a tractor which then pulled the walls down. But it is a shame the castle was not preserved for future generations as some other castles were in other Irish towns, like Dalkey.

Top left: A 1927 photo of Little Bray and the castle;
Far left: The four-arched bridge over the Dargle painted in 1847 by Bartlett, note the castle on the then recently new Castle Street;
Left: Castle Street in 1972, the castle would have been situated in the grassy area on the right of the photo.

BRAY – DID YOU KNOW...?

County Wicklow · Ireland

braydidyouknow@gmail.com

Pillars of local history

Next time you are posting a letter in Bray, take a look at the post box that you are posting it in. Chances are that it is quite old...perhaps very, very old! Bray has a fine collection of traditional letter and pillar boxes dating from the 19th century and early 20th century. These handsome items make for a very attractive and familiar part of the Irish street scene.

Most bear witness to a time when the postal service was a much more critical element in daily communications. Hence the older parts of the town are relatively well served with boxes while one can look hard and long for one elsewhere.

For example, the nearest place residents of Diamond Valley and Dargle Road (West) can post a letter is in the pillar box on the Lower Dargle Road. This one, like the box on Albert Avenue, bears the emblem of King Edward the Seventh (ERVII), while the post box at the old Courthouse (beside Bray Bridge) displays the monogram of his mother the redoubtable Queen Victoria (VR). Others display his son King George the Fifth (GRV).

A fine example is located on Sidmonton Road. This is a rare Penfold design, named after the architect who designed it in 1866. Penfold-style boxes are found in Ireland and England and there are examples all over the former British Empire including India and Australia.

A more thorough look at the base of the pillarbox on Main Street – opposite Holland's pub – the manufacturer's name 'A. Handyside & Co. Ltd. Derby & London' is visible. Andrew Handyside and Company also built the Friar Gate Bridge in Derby, England. There are obviously no boxes bearing the cipher of any British monarchs after George V as Ireland began to issue its own distinctive designs after 1922 – initially as Saorstat Eireann or SE, then the P7T logo (Posts & Telegraphs which was abolished in 1984) familiar to people of a certain vintage and most recently as simply An Post.

Even these later versions though owe a lot to the original design – including the colour. Yes, the original British pillar box of the 1850s was painted green to help them blend in. This was eventually changed to red after about 25 years in response to complaints that they were too hard to see! It just goes to show how much history and stories lie behind some of the simplest items around our town of Bray – items which we take for granted every day.

Clockwise from top left: The P7T box in the Vevay; this post box is in the wall below the old courthouse it displays the VR (Queen Victoria) emblem; the 'Handyside & Co.' box on Main Street; the rare 1866 Penfold-style pillar (and its emblem) on Sidmonton Road; the emblem of King Edward the Seventh (and its emblem) on the postbox at the Dargle Road, there is also one of the same at Albert Avenue.

BRAY- DID YOU KNOW...?

County Wicklow · Ireland

braydidyouknow@gmail.com

POSTCARDS FROM BRAY

Railway Station, Bray, Co. Wicklow. c.1910.

Ray O'Donnell

The second of three postcards of Bray Railway Station. Note the old signal box on the right.

40

BRAY – DID YOU KNOW...?

County Wicklow · Ireland

braydidyouknow@gmail.com

The Bray Head Aerial Chair-Lifts (Part I of II)

In 1946 Eamon Quinn's (father of supermarket chain owner Fergal Quinn) ambition of a holiday camp on Bray Head was coming to fruition. His company - *Irish Holidays Limited* - purchased the *Eagle's Nest* and Mr. Quinn was determined to make it an even more popular place than it already was.

The *Eagle's Nest* was one of the top spots in Bray in the 1930s and 1940s – a wonderful café which boasted breathtaking views by day and a very popular ballroom by night. However, the *Eagle's Nest* being located mid-way up Bray Head was not an easy place to get to, in fact the only way to get there from the seafront was by walking up a pathway and then the 47 steep steps which were adjacent to the old church ruins – and this was not an easy task for some. Of course you could always get the *Bray Head Express*, which was generally a horse pulled cart, but this would have limited seating and would cost you 6d. per person.

Eamon Quinn's idea of an aerial cableway system was way before its time, and he was sure that it would, not only attract visitors to ride on the lifts, but many more people would visit his new venture at the Eagle's Nest. So his wife and himself set off to Switzerland to visit some cable cars and chair-lifts in action and was very happy with what he saw, and by 1951 *Irish Holidays Ltd* were the proud owners of the Bray Head Aerial Chair-Lift.

This was not only a new venture in Ireland, but was the only one of its kind in Great Britain too. The chair–lifts became a great amenity and attracted tourists in their hundreds. A day out in Bray wasn't fulfilled until you went to the Eagle's Nest on the chair-lifts.

THE EAGLE'S NEST

Cafe and Ballroom

BRAY HEAD

Magnificent Panoramic Views of the Coastline and Countryside

Delicious meals in pleasant surroundings

Public Dancing

Modern Snack Bar and Soda Fountain

Wine Licence

Enjoy an exhilarating ride on

THE AERIAL CHAIR-LIFT

TO THE EAGLE'S NEST

The only one of its kind in Great Britain and Ireland.

Left: The Bray Head Express at the Eagle's Nest;
Top right: The chair-lifts during the 60s;
Right: A flyer for the Eagle's Nest and the Aerial Chair-Lifts.

© Bray – Did You Know 2012

41

The Bray Head Aerial Chair-Lifts (Part II of II)

There's fun ahead at Bray Head go gay all the way on Ireland's only

Aerial Cableway

take in the most breathtaking view you've ever seen!!

The AERIAL CABLEWAY STARTS ITS LIFT UP — FROM THE BOTTOM OF BRAY HEAD AT THE END OF THE PROMENADE

on your way to the

★ EAGLE'S NEST BALLROOM

Tea Room, Snack Bar, Novelty Mini Golf Course

But the new transport scheme had its teething problems, notably the wind factor. The chair-lifts could not operate in strong winds and the system used electric power, and it would often 'break down', leaving people sitting high up on the chair-lifts until they were repaired. Special engineers had to be summoned and this was not only expensive, but it sometimes took hours to get the chair-lifts up and running again. Jimmy Coleman, who ran the aerial chair-lifts turned out better than any engineer in the end and after a while – it was a rare incident that the system would fail.

The views of Bray and beyond were magnificent from the chairlifts and safety was paramount. People were well strapped into the chair and nobody ever fell off, in fact, in all the years of operation there was never a serious incident. The lifts ran from a platform – which is still in existence – adjacent to the car park at Raheen Park to the terminus at the Eagle's Nest Café, which is 137 meters above sea level. The carrying capacity was 300 people per hour each way. There were 14 cars each which could carry two adults side-by-side and spaced 48 yards apart. The chair-lift traveled along 7 pylons, which carried the cable at varying heights from the ground due to the contour of the land.

Irish Holidays Limited eventually sold the Eagle's Nest and the Bray Head Aerial Chair-Lifts ceased operations in 1976. But if you remember being on the chair-lifts it's a memory to treasure; if you never took a ride on them...you missed an opportunity which will never arise again.

Top right: A couple decend on the cableway; right: some of the pylons used to carry the cable; far right: the terminus at the car park as it is today. One would eagerly wait here for their turn for a ride up the mountain on the chair-lift.

BRAY – DID YOU KNOW…?

County Wicklow · Ireland

braydidyouknow@gmail.com

Bray… the past in pictures

TOWN OF BRAY.

43

BRAY - DID YOU KNOW...?

County Wicklow · Ireland

braydidyouknow@gmail.com

In the 1960s, Status Quo were one of the great bands who played at 'The Arcadia' in Bray. The Arcadia was situated behind the International Hotel and became 'The Fillmore West' Club in the early 1970s. Many top acts played there including The Yardbirds – the site is now the unoccupied building (below) opposite the DART station.

44

BRAY – DID YOU KNOW...?

County Wicklow · Ireland

braydidyouknow@gmail.com

INTO THE WEST

MADE IN BRAY

MY BOY JACK

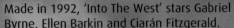

Made in 1992, 'Into The West' stars Gabriel Byrne, Ellen Barkin and Ciarán Fitzgerald.

Did you know...
- that Ellen Barkin and Gabriel Byrne were married to each other when 'Into The West' was made.

- in the movie, neither boy can read until Tito gets a few lessons, but still can't read well, however, when the horse takes them to their mother's grave Ossie, who has not learned to read, asks "Why is my birthday on that stone?"

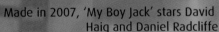

Made in 2007, 'My Boy Jack' stars David Haig and Daniel Radcliffe

Did you know...
- several scenes of 'My Boy Jack' were shot at the actual Rudyard Kipling Estate, Bateman's, where Kipling lived from 1902 until his death.

- many of the photos of wounded men that the Kipling family search through clearly show a WW2 pattern 'Brodie' steel helmet. Not only is a WW2 steel helmet wrong, ANY steel helmet is wrong for late 1915 as steel helmets weren't issued to British troops until 1916.

BRAY – DID YOU KNOW...?

County Wicklow · Ireland

braydidyouknow@gmail.com

The B&ER (Bray to Enniskerry Railway) *Part I of III*

Between 1840 and 1910, more than a dozen proposals were put forward to link the village of Enniskerry to the town of Bray by rail or tramway. Some never developed beyond a gleam in the eye of an entrepreneur, while others got bogged down in the complicated legal and political procedures involved in seeking approval for any new rail or tramway scheme. But in the end, the plan didn't succeed.

However, construction did begin on the railway, substantial parts of the engineering structures of the line were built and these include a bridge built to carry the railway over Dublin Corporation's Vartry watermain on the Bray Road from Enniskerry to the N11, which remains to this day (Wicklow County Council removed a lot of the railway embankment in the 2007 road widening scheme, but made a policy decision to leave the bridge, which is directly opposite the ornate bridge carrying the watermain over the Cookstown River, a tributary of the Dargle).

So why was there such an interest in a railway line between Bray and the village of Enniskerry? The promoters hoped to open up the entire Powerscourt area – from Glencree to Carrigolligan and from the Sugar Loaf to the Scalp – enhancing the development of

An artist's view of a train leaving Bray station. The narrow strip between the rails and the Carlisle Grounds on the right was to have been used for the Bray and Enniskerry railway line and terminal.

agriculture and tourism. A railway or tramway would provide a rapid and cost-effective way of exporting agricultural produce, and of importing bulk consumer goods. Increased efficiency in agricultural production would enhance the wealth of the area for both landowners and the local population. Increased incomes could be spent on an expanded choice of imported consumer goods, ranging from building materials for improving housing, through coal for warming the middle-class and upper-class residences, to a variety of household goods and equipment which could be stocked locally rather than being available only in Bray. Horses and carts were the only available transport for bringing tourists or moving goods and these were slow, costly to hire and capable of carrying only small loads. After a few years of the arrival of the railway to Bray, a building boom in hotels and tourist facilities converted Bray into a large-scale holiday resort. So, at the time, a Bray to Enniskerry railway line made good sense. The arrival of a new railway could transform the whole personality of the area.

Above: Ladies wait at Bray Station for transport to Enniskerry – then the only means of getting there.

to be continued...

The B&ER (Bray to Enniskerry Railway) *Part II of III*

In 1860 a proposal had been put forward for a steam railway service to link Bray and Enniskerry. Nothing materialized on the project until 1866 when an Act of Parliament was passed which gave parliamentary approval to construct the Bray and Enniskerry Light Railway.

This 1866 route for the railway line would see trains leaving Bray from a new terminus (other proposals had the train leaving Bray railway station), which was to have been built at the spot where Fatima House on the Quinsborough Road is now, but running on a separate track along the lane that runs between the main railway line and the Carlisle Grounds (as on the illustration on Part I) and curving as it passed by the area where the sewage treatment plant is now located. The curve would then reach the river bank – below left – (where Seapoint Court is situated now) and the track was to continue along what is now the riverside walk towards Bray Bridge. Here the line was to pass through the side-arch of the bridge on the Main Street side. A halt-stop was to be built to serve the Main Street and Little Bray areas at the spot on the riverwalk against Bray Bridge – where the steps at the old Courthouse are now.

Bray Bridge was one of the biggest engineering obstructions encountered by the company. To meet the requirement of avoiding any obstruction to the flow of the river under the bridge, the track level had to be elevated, perhaps being carried on a seperate bridge at right angles to Bray Bridge above. Yet the height of the trains required substantial headroom. The solution proposed was the replacement of the granite side-arch of Bray Bridge with a metal span – 'with iron girders and a flat arch' – like, for example, the railway bridge at Albert Avenue, which would have given more space above the track than the existing arch. The agreement to allow this reconstruction of the bridge led to recriminations in the Bray Urban District Council at a later date. Beyond the bridge, a track would have veered to the right, bridging the mill race which formerly flowed along the Mill Lane and discharged into the mainstream of the Dargle River just above the bridge – as many people will remember.

to be continued...

Top left: the remnants of the half-stop beside the arch for the railway line at Bray Bridge. Above: the riverbank at the People's Park.

BRAY - DID YOU KNOW...?

The B&ER (Bray to Enniskerry Railway) *Part III of III*

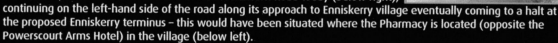

The track was then designed to hug the river bank running between the buildings and the river past the People's Park and Commons (top right) as far as Kilcroney. After reaching Kilcroney Cross, the line would turn at a forty-five-degree angle under the (N11) road (top left) in a tunnel towards the Enniskerry junction and follow the Lower Cookstown Road on its north side as far as the Big Tree (just past the entrance to Powerscourt).

Just beyond the Big Tree, a bridge was to carry the railway line over the road to an embankment hugging the

road on its south side. The line would continue over the bridge erected to take the weight of the permanent way off the Dublin Corporation (now Dublin City Council) water main, which still stands on the Lower Cookstown Road today (below right), continuing on the left-hand side of the road along its approach to Enniskerry village eventually coming to a halt at the proposed Enniskerry terminus – this would have been situated where the Pharmacy is located (opposite the Powerscourt Arms Hotel) in the village (below left).

Construction on the system began on just one undertaking and was 'proceeding very satisfactorily' until unforeseen financial problems, arising from a partnership with a shady finance company, brought the work to a sudden stop. The result was an unfinished railway which was a target of vandalism and a focus for litigation. Creditors scrambled to recover their assets as the track, only recently laid, was ripped up again and sold off. The less-easily liquidated features - the embankments and cuttings, and the walls and bridges - soon began to decay.

In 1900 the commissioners proposed trams for Bray and intended to connect this system with the Bray and Enniskerry line. Around this period there were schemes for tramway in various parts of Wicklow, including

Enniskerry to Hollybrook, Glendalough to Hollybrook, and Dundrum to Enniskerry and Bray. Today very few remnants remain to remind us of the vision and hopes of the Victorian entrepreneurs.

But was a railway from Bray to Enniskerry ever going to work? Would the investors have ever made financial profit from such a scheme? It doesn't seem likely, after all would Veolia Transport, who operate the LUAS, run a tram system from Bray to Enniskerry today? One would have to think not.

Murder on Bray Commons

On the evening of 31st December 1767, a poor woman who travelled around the country with a showbox and a 'dancing' dog was found murdered in the most inhuman manner on the commons in Bray. The Bray Commons was more or less the area of land that streched from the sea along the north side of the Dargle River as far as the Blind Lane. The Coroners inquest sat and brought in a verdict of 'Wilful murder by persons unknown'.

A young drummer was later arrested on suspicion of the woman's murder.

Top right: The People's Park on the Lower Dargle Road was part of the Bray Commons. Bottom right: A photo of the Commons area c. 1890 - back in 1767 there was very little housing on the Commons.

49

A fine quality photograph of Castle Street and Little Bray (south) c. 1890. The photo, taken from Dublin Road opposite Ravenswell clearly shows the tower of the old castle – demolished in 1937 – which can be seen to the left of the photo and to the right of the tower is the old court house – its roof can be seen in the above photo. Back Street and the entrance to Sheridan's Lane are also visible (centre of photo), both roads now long gone. Castle Street was constructed as a bye-pass for Little Bray and Back Street in c. 1808, before then one would pass over the bridge and down a very hard left bend onto Back Street and on to the Dublin Road.

Thomas Oldham and the Oldhamia Radiata of Bray Head

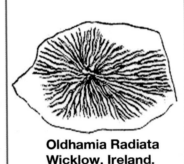

**Oldhamia Radiata
Wicklow, Ireland.**

Thomas Oldham (4 May 1816, Dublin - 17 July 1878, Rugby, England) was a Anglo-Irish geologist. He was educated at Trinity College, Dublin and studied civil engineering at the University of Edinburgh as well as geology under Robert Jameson.

In 1838 he joined the Ordnance Survey in Ireland as a chief assistant under Joseph Ellison Portlock who was studying the geology of Londonderry and neighbourhood. Portlock wrote of him *"whenever I have required his aid, I have found him possessed of the highest intelligence and the most unbounded zeal"*.

Thomas Oldham
(1816–1878)

Oldham discovered radiating fan–shaped impressions on Bray Head in 1840. He showed this to the English palaeontologist Edward Forbes, who named it 'Oldhamia' after Thomas Oldham. These were – at the time – considered the oldest fossils in the world.

Oldham became Curator to the Geological Society of Dublin, and in 1845 succeeded John Phillips, nephew of William Smith, in the Chair of Geology at Trinity College, Dublin. He was elected a Fellow of the Royal Society in June 1848 and in 1850, he married Louisa Matilda Dixon of Liverpool.

After resigning in November of that year, he took a position as the first Superintendent of the Geological Survey of India. Thomas Oldham was to be the first of the Irish geologists to migrate to the Subcontinent.

He was followed by his brother Charles William King, and by more than twelve other Irish geologists.

'Cheiro' - the Bray Clairvoyant

In the early years of the 20th century one of Ireland's greatest clairvoyants predicted the future of countless thousands of people across the world, many of whom were famous.

This was the great "Cheiro" (pronounced ki-ro) otherwise known as Count Louis Le Warner Harmon. He was born on November 1, 1866 in Bray, Co. Wicklow and was christened William John Warner.

In the years to come he became one of the most famous palmists and clairvoyants that the world has ever known, he used palmistry, astrology, and Chaldean numerology, to make startlingly accurate predictions, including world events. He read some 25,000 hands, among them such celebrities as King Edrvard VII, Lord Kitchener, Thomas Edison, William Gladstone, Lillie Langtry, Mark Twain and Oscar Wilde and many others. He wrote many books and he foresaw the sinking of the Titanic and actually warned the journalist W.T. Stead, not to travel by water during the month of April, 1912. Stead ignored the advice, and was drowned when the Titanic sank on her maiden voyage to New York on April 15th. 1912, with the loss of 1,517 lives.

Cheiro acquired his expertise in India. As a teenager, he traveled to the Bombay port of Apollo Bunder. There, he met his Guru, an Indian Brahmin, who took him to his village in the valley of the Konkan region of Maharashtra to study. Although considered to be a 'chancer' by some, his predictions made him a celebrity with kings, rulers and millionaires, who became his clients and who seldom doubted his occult powers. Cheiro was tall, handsome, broad shouldered and distinguished looking. Women were attracted to him, fascinated by his dark eyes, and his deep voice with its slight Irish lilt.

He spent his final years in Hollywood, seeing as many as 20 clients a day before his death on October 8, 1936, in Hollywood, California, at the age of 69. His own ghost is reported to have appeared after his death at his California home in Hollywood where he died. This house is well known for being haunted, and in 1976 the tenants reported extraordinary noises and even saw apparitions there. Cheiro had requested a simple funeral, but instead he was given a true Hollywood send off. As he lay on a bed of fresh roses, his fellow countryman, count John McCormac sang *"I Hear you Calling Me"*.

Top right: One of Cheiro's books; bottom: Cheiro's Indian Room.

The Turkish Baths (Part I of III)

The Turkish Baths – or later known as The Bray Assembly Rooms – were situated halfway down the Quinsborough Road, the *Boulevard Centre* is on the exact spot today. Built in 1859, Bray at this time was in the grip of a building boom: the railway to Dublin had been opened five years before, and a group of businessmen were engaged in transforming the existing small sea-bathing town into a major seaside resort on the English pattern.

The Turkish Baths were designed by Mr Richard Barter, architect nephew of the owner of St Ann's Hydropathic Establishment. Owned by the wealthy businessman William Dargan and operated under the supervision of Dr Richard Barter, they were officially opened by the earl of Meath on 15th October 1859, and a fortnight later to the public.

The building was 180ft long by 70ft wide (55m x 21m approx.), the base was of cut granite from the quarries at Dalkey and the walls were of red and white bricks, laid in an ornate chequered pattern, with tall minarets at the corners. At the back there was a 70ft-high ornamental chimney to disperse the fumes from the coke-fed furnace. The main entrance faced the Quinsborough Road, with lesser entrances at either end to the east and west 'wings'.

But the building must have been quite beautiful and exquisite – inside and out – as Robert Wollaston (who published important works on Roman baths) described the baths as follows:
"The building cost £10,000; it is extremely handsome, of an Oriental style of architecture of red and white bricks alternately placed, and faced with stone. The interior is very appropriately decorated, and composed of several apartments admirably adapted to their respective uses. The ceiling is painted in arabesque, and richly colored with the favorite Turkish colours green, red, and blue. The windows are all of colored glass, and the light of the apartment is most agreeably diffused by the hues of the glass. The centre is ornamented with a handsome marble fountain; flowers and aquatic plants, and ferns, interspersed amongst shells and rock-work, adorn the fountain."

to be continued...

Top left: A colour photo of the building; inset right: William Dargan, who owned the Turkish Baths; Right centre: The baths in all its glory before the brick patterns were obliterated c. 1880; Below Right: The building as the Bray Assembly Rooms.

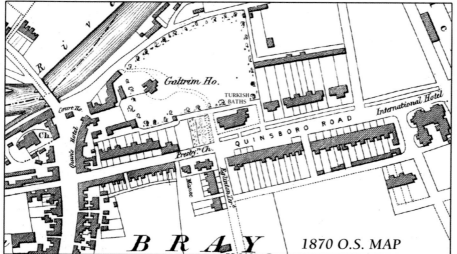

1870 O.S. MAP

© Bray - Did You Know 2012

BRAY - DID YOU KNOW...?

County Wicklow · Ireland

braydidyouknow@gmail.com

A bird's eye view - now and then...

The Turkish Baths were situated on the Quinsborough Road on the site where the Boulevard Shopping Centre is today.

Top left is a photo from Google Earth showing the town centre and Quinsborough Road - the site is clearly marked.

Below left is an 1870 Ordnance Survey map of the same area with the Turkish Baths centre. Note that Galtrim Park (road left of the Baths) had not been extended to join the Seapoint Road as it does today.

A ground plan from the 1870 Ordnance Survey map (below) shows the Turkish Baths / Assembly Rooms building in detail. Original scale 10 feet to the mile.

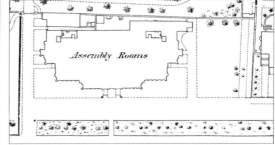

The Turkish Baths (Part II of III)

Wollaston continued: *"The flooring is richly inlaid with tesselated pavement - made for the purpose at Minton's Porcelain Works, in Staffordshire - in imitation of the pavement of ancient Baths. The warm and hot air rooms are also beautifully constructed, with marble seats and tesselated pavement; the domes are enriched with stars of variegated glass, which give a brilliant appearance. There are, in recesses connected with the hot rooms, chambers for ablution, where tepid and cold water are plentifully supplied as Shower and Dash Baths; and there are to be attendants in Turkish costume to shampoo the bathers; coffee and sherbet, cigars and pipes, will be added, to complete the whole ceremony of the Turkish mode of bathing."*

Bray's Turkish Baths opened to the public on 2nd November 1859. The opening hours were from 6am to 11pm, except for Sundays, when the baths closed for five hours in the middle of the day. There was a choice of public or private bathing, and bathing dresses, sheets and towels were included in the charge of two shillings or three shillings respectively. Shampooing cost sixpence extra, but was not available on Sundays. But it is hard to imagine that the baths were ever full of bathers even that first winter. Bray's summer visitors were long gone, and although for the first few weeks curious Dubliners probably travelled out by train, this journey was very quickly made unnecessary when Dr Barter opened Turkish baths in Lincoln Place, Dublin, in February 1860.

To make matters worse, a major attack on the use of dry rather than humid air in the new Turkish baths appeared in the medical press in January 1860, using the baths at 'B***' as an example. The writer claimed that the dry air aggravated his sciatica rather than alleviating it, and that the treatment was actually dangerous to patients. There was a further allegation that in Bray the hot air contained fumes from the coke furnace. The controversy raged, not only in the medical press but also more widely, with Dr Barter and his supporters indignantly refuting the criticisms.

to be continued...

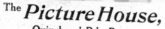

Clockwise from left: The derelict building c. 1968; A old advert for 'Mac's Picture House'; A photo of the west front side of the building.

Left: An advert for the Turkish Baths in Waterford, also ran by Dr. Barter (centre).

Turkish Baths,

QUINSBOROUGH ROAD, BRAY.
JUST MINUTES FROM THE TRAIN STATION

• • •

IN consequence of the long-continued success of this Bath, and to still further popularize and extend its benign influence, and in accordance with the spirit of the times, the proprietor has determined to adopt the following

REDUCED PRICES:

Baths, singly, £1.00 ; Six Tickets, £5.00.

OPEN FROM 6 A.M. TO 11 P.M. JANUARY 1, 1871.

THE IMPROVED TURKISH

IRISH BATH,

UNDER DOCTOR BARTER'S PATENT.

HARDY'S ROAD, WATERFORD,

Open on Week Days.

FIRST CLASS.

From 6 to Half-past 8 a.m.
From Half ... d p.m.
From 0 ...
Children ...
Sub ...

TO ... THE MILLION

ON ... P.M.

... 9 A.M.,

NO ... ALLOWED.

The interior of the Turkish Baths at Limerick was very similar to Bray.

TURKISH BATH—SUDATORIUM OR HOT ROOM.

THE IMPROVED TURKISH

Or ROMAN BATHS

A side door at the Turkish Baths: Note the brickwork where the plaster has fallen.

The Turkish Baths (Part III of III)

Meanwhile other Turkish baths had been opened by Dr Barter in towns and cities across Ireland. Most of these were purpose-built and, like Bray's baths, in Moorish style. But despite this surge in interest countrywide Bray's Turkish baths were not a success. In the winter of 1862 bathers were offered free entry, and by 1864 Dargan was trying unsuccessfully to sell the baths for £4,000.

By this time the baths were closed, and they were never again to operate as intended. In 1867 a new company converted the building into assembly rooms for concerts and other entertainments, although Dr Barter reopened Turkish baths in one of the 'wings', presumably using some of the original small bath rooms and chambers.

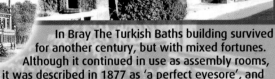

In Bray The Turkish Baths building survived for another century, but with mixed fortunes. Although it continued in use as assembly rooms, it was described in 1877 as 'a perfect eyesore', and later as a 'speckled elephant' (as opposed to a white one); in about 1900 the exterior was rendered, obliterating the brick patterns. In the early twentieth century it became a cinema, known as 'Mac's Cinema', but finally the building stood derelict, a sad ghost, until the demolition squad arrived in December 1979. Now a small, undistinguished shopping precinct occupies the site. But like 'Naylor's Cove' and Little Bray Castle, if the baths building had survived just a little longer, the current interest in preservation might have assisted in its rescue - to the great enrichment of Bray's architectural heritage.

Left & Top: The Turkish Baths just before the bulldozers moved in to demolish it; Inset: A drawing of the baths in all its glory from 'Heffernan's Illustrated Plan of Bray'.

POSTCARDS FROM BRAY

Railway Station, Bray, Co. Wicklow. c.1905

Ray O'Donnell

The third of three postcards of Bray Railway Station - years before the east platform was built.

BRAY – DID YOU KNOW...?

County Wicklow · Ireland

FAMOUS BRAY PEOPLE

Eddie Jordan

Multi-millionaire Eddie Jordan was born in Bray, Co. Wicklow in 1948. Ex-racing driver and founder of the Jordan Formula One Racing Team, Eddie's wife, Marie, is an ex-All Ireland Under-18 basketball player. The couple have four children.

Their main base is in Ireland where Jordan keeps his personal helicopter, and he also has homes in Wentworth, South Kinsington, London and in Monaco, where he keeps his yacht.

Paul McNaughton

Paul McNaughton was an Irish rugby union, soccer and GAA player during the 1970s and 1980s. He played rugby as a centre, with Leinster, Ireland, Greystones and Wanderers. Between 1978 and 1981, McNaughton won 15 caps for Ireland.

Although better known as a rugby player, he also played soccer for both Shelbourne F.C. and Bray Wanderers A.F.C. Born in 1952, McNaughton - originally from the Palermo area of Little Bray - represented Wicklow GAA in both senior football and minor hurling, making him the only person to play three sports in Ireland's national stadiums.

Bray Bridge from Ravenswell Road today and a postcard from the early 20th Century from nearly the same spot. The old barracks building (far right) is still there, but covered by trees in the modern photo. The old tower of the Holy Redeemer Church can also be seen right of the old Courthouse (right) and the new tower is above. The ruins of the building at the river was to be a stop point for passengers using the Bray to Enniskerry Railway line, which would have passed along the river bank and on under the south arch to Enniskerry. But the plan never materialised.

BRAY – DID YOU KNOW...?

County Wicklow · Ireland

braydidyouknow@gmail.com

The White Coons

Early in 1891 Clifford Essex, a singer and banjo player, was so impressed with a troupe of Pierrot entertainers during a visit to France that he formed a group himself. He obtained his first booking in Bray in 1891 and so Ireland which was still under British rule became the first place in the British Isles to feature a Pierrot concert party.

Will C. Pepper, who began his career with Essex, formed his own troupe, 'The White Coons and Banjo Troupe' in 1899 and played in Bray for many years, mostly performing on the small bandstand opposite Lacy's (now the Esplanade Hotel) which was reserved for visiting variety shows. Stanley Holloway, famous for his comic and character roles on stage and screen, especially that of Alfred P. Doolittle in *My Fair Lady*, began his career with

Peppers' Coons. Jack McDermott, who later owned the Arcadia Ballroom and Mac's Cinema (at the old Turkish Baths) performed with the Coons, as did Mike NoNo ('The Man with the Twinkling Feet'). Also appearing in Bray at that period were, 'The George Rappel Troupe', 'The Harcourt and Filbert Troupe', George Carey, 'The Celtic Glee Singers' and 'The Argyle Minstrels'.

WILL C. PEPPER'S "WHITE COONS" BRAY 1906.

The 'White Coons' posing for a photo at Killick's studio in Bray in 1906. Back L to R: James Godden, Allan Thomas, Alf Wood. Front L to R: Ada Watson, May Windsor. Top right: The Coons performing on the bandstand opposite the Esplanade Hotel. Below right: Pepper 'Botling', that is collecting among the audience on the Esplanade.

RELIGIOUS PROCESSIONS

1954: A First Holy Communion procession on Castle Street.

1930s: A procession passes Brighton Terrace and the Town Hall.

A procession on Convent Avenue.

A Corpus Christi procession on Main Street c. 1947.

Passing Delimata's and Donwear, Main Street c. 1955.

A May procession on the Quinsboro' Road c. 1955.

The Arcadia: Bray's Ballroom of Romance (Part I of II)

Jack McDermott – who also owned Mac's Picture House at the Turkish Baths – took a lease on the Arcadia Dance Pavilion and its beautiful gardens in the early years of the last century. The interior of the Arcadia in the 1940s and 50s was magnificent. The ceiling was wooden and had many rotating mirror balls, which would reflect the coloured lights onto the dancers on the dance floor. Those who were not taking part in the dancing would sit on the red velvet-clad chairs, which surrounded the exquisite maple dance floor.

Outside the Arcadia there was an iron railing which ran right around the perimeter of the building, and it wasn't an unusual sight to see an outside audience standing watching the great dancers strut their stuff as they passed by the large glass windows.

The Arcadia - which was the first ever cabaret in Ireland - boasted having the top international orchestras of the 1940s and 1950s, bands such as Harrison's Famous Band, The Oriental Dance Orchestra, the Clipper Carltons, Billy Carter and his band with Rose Tynan, Malachy Sweeney Band, the Jim Bacon Orchestra, Neil Kearns, The Moonglows and The Dixielanders. Brendan Boyer and Joe Loss and his orchestra.

Jack McDermott eventually sold the Arcadia to Alex Corscadden, a very popular businessman from Kilcock - whose family owned the International Hotel until 1962 - but the Arcadia burned down in 1962. The land was then sold to a group of Dublin businessmen and after many months of re-building, the Arcadia opened again, only this time it was a lot bigger...

Top: The 'Oriental Band' at the Arcadia c. 1920.
Far left: The Bray Hunt Ball, Christmas 1940.
Left: The demolition of the Arcadia after the fire in 1962.

BRAY – DID YOU KNOW...?

County Wicklow · Ireland

braydidyouknow@gmail.com

The Arcadia: Bray's Ballroom of Romance *(Part II of II)*

The 1960s brought top dance bands and cabaret artists such as The Hollies, The Tremolos, Marmalade, Roy Orbison, Mary Hopkins, The Move, P.J. Proby, Status Quo, Mungo Gerry, Scott McKenzie, Tom Jones, The Troggs, Englebert Humperdink, Lulu, The Every Brothers, Sandy Shaw, Manfred Mann, Donovan, The Searches and Rod Stewart to the Arcadia, but its days as a dancehall were numbered. Times were changing, it was the eve of the 1970s and other top music venues were opening around the country.

As the Christmas of 1969 drew near, it was becoming very obvious that all the efforts of the **'Save The Arcadia Committee'** to have the building utilized as a community centre were doomed, the Town Engineer stating *"that a considerable sum of money would be required to put the building in order"*. The Department of Local Government had indicated that there would be no money available for this project. A sum of £170,000 was quoted as being the estimated cost of purchasing the building and carrying out the badly needed repairs and refurbishment – and so ended the story of the Arcadia as a centre for entertainment.

During its metamorphosis as the *Filmore West* which opened in 1972, the popular club played host to top groups such as The Who, Thin Lizzy, Horslips, Planxty and Van Morrison, and many more, but it didn't last long, English bands were apprehensive about visiting Ireland during the troubles in Northern Ireland and the club closed for good in 1973.

The building was used for popular Bingo nights for a few years after, and then lay dormant. Eventually being turned into a 'Cash & Carry' business – the featureless building now lies dormant once again, reflecting nothing of what a legendary dance hall that it once was.

Top left: The late Jimmy Saville joins the Miami Showband as guest on stage at the Arcadia.
Left Centre: Roy Orbison and Olive Plunket at the Arcadia c. 1968.
Left and right: Various adverts and flyers for the Arcadia through the years..

— COME TO OUR —
POINT - TO - POINT DANCE
— AT —
ARCADIA : : BRAY
THIS EVENING
10 p.m. to 3 a.m.

Peter Keogh's Dance Band

Tickets ... 5/- each
Including Tax and Running Buffet : : *Evening Dress Optional*

The Bright Spot in Ireland
ARCADIA
PAVILION and GARDENS
(opposite the Railway Station)
13th Successive Season of
Summer Seaside Dances
Two Ballroom Floors–Outside & Inside
Harrison's Famous Band.

ARCADIA
NEW
Pavilion and Gardens.
High-class Vaudeville Entertainments
Twice Daily, at 3.30 and 7.45.

© Bray – Did You Know 2012

BRAY - DID YOU KNOW...?

County Wicklow · Ireland

braydidyouknow@gmail.com

LACEYS HOTEL AND ESPLANADE, BRAY, CO. WICKLOW.

Esplanade... (White Coons) Co. Wicklow.

Past Postcards from Bray Seafront

Bray Co. Wicklow.

(Above) A great shot of the Quinsborough Road (looking towards Main Street) in the 50s...Harvey's and the Post Office on the right. (Right) The fire brigade attend to a fire at the Coach & Horses Pub on the Dublin Road in Little Bray c. 1952.

BRAY in the **50s!**

BRAY – DID YOU KNOW...?

County Wicklow · Ireland

braydidyouknow@gmail.com

The 'Oldcourt Scheme' - Wolfe Tone Square

As a result of a survey carried out in Bray in 1927 by the Medical Office of Health and the Town Surveyor, upwards of 700 then existing dwellings (mostly in the Little Bray area) were certified as being unfit for human habitation. A programme of gradual clearance and rebuilding was embarked upon and by 1935 200 families had been re-housed in the new cottage homes.

The scheme, officially known as the 'Oldcourt Scheme', was laid out to accommodate 161 four-roomed and 100 three-roomed, two-storey cottages, each with gardens front and rear, and with hot and cold water supplies.

The O'Byrne Road Scheme started in 1927 and by 1935 the new houses of Wolfe Tone Square were well under way and nearly complete. The Grotto in Wolfe Tone was built in 1954.

Top right: The painters who worked on the scheme.
Right: The Grotto in the middle of the estate.
Far right: Plasterers who worked on the scheme c. 1935.
Below left: The 1934 original plan of the Oldcourt Scheme.
Below middle and right: The site in preparation for the 261 homes c. 1933 and a photo today from the same spot.

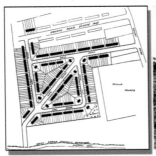

c. 1933

2011

67

The Miami Showband

The Miami Showband was one of the great Irish showbands, fronted at their peak by the charismatic figure of Dickie Rock, then Bray's Fran O'Toole (above center). Songs such as 'There's Always Me', 'I'm Yours' and 'From the Candy Store on the Corner' gave the band consecutive number one hits, and secured their position as one of Ireland's premier bands.

But on the morning of 31 July, 1975 the band were on their way home from a gig in Banbridge, County Down, when they were stopped at a bogus military checkpoint resulting in the massacre of three of the band members.

This is their story...

The 'Miami Showband Massacre' (Part I of III)

One of the first photos of The Miami Showband, c. 1963. Front: Joe Tyrrell. Seated: Tommy O'Rourke, Clem Quinn, Tony Bogan, Tony Harris, Murty Quinn. Standing: Dickie Rock, Martin Phelan.

The Miami Showband were one of the most successful and popular showbands in Ireland in the 1960s and 1970s. Led at first by singer Dickie Rock, and later by Fran O'Toole, they had seven number one records on the Irish singles chart.

The band was established in Dublin in 1962 by impresario Tom Doherty. He recruited an existing group, the Downbeats Quartet, comprising Joe Tyrell (piano), Tony Bogan (drums), Clem Quinn (guitar), and Martin Phelan (saxophone), and augmented them with singer Dickie Rock (at the time, a member of another group, the Melochords), trumpeter Tommy O'Rourke, trombonist and vocalist Murty Quinn, and bass player Denis Murray. The group's first engagement was at the Palm Beach Ballroom in Portmarnock, and so they were named the Miami Showband. They rapidly became one of the top showbands in the country, and their first single, a version of the Elvis Presley album track *"There's Always Me"* reached number one in the Irish charts in December 1963. They had four further number one hits over the next two years: *"I'm Yours"* and *"From the Candy Store on the Corner"* (both 1964), and *"Every Step of the Way"* and *"Wishing It Was You"* (both 1965). *"Every Step of the Way"* was the first song by an Irish artist to go straight in as a number one single in the Irish charts. In 1966, they were chosen to sing Ireland's entry in the Eurovision Song Contest, and their song *"Come Back To Stay"* also reached the top of the charts. They also appeared on British TV, on Sunday Night at the London Palladium and Thank Your Lucky Stars.

The Miami Showband are joined on stage by special guest Jimmy Saville at the Arcadia, Bray in the 1960s.

In 1967, four members of the band – Murty Quinn, Joe Tyrell, Denis Murray and Martin Phelan – split away to form their own group, The Sands. They were replaced by songwriter and singer Fran O'Toole, Paul Ashford, Pat McCarthy, Des Lee (born Des McAlea) and Brian McCoy. The group's final number one came with "Simon Says" (a version of the 1910 Fruitgum Company song) in 1968. McCarthy and Tony Bogan later left, and were replaced by Danny Ellis and Martin Brannigan. The group released an album, *The Wind Will Change Tomorrow*, in 1970.

The "new" Miami in 1967, soon after some members left to form The Sands. Front: Clem Quinn, Brian McCoy, Des Lee, Fran O'Toole, Dickie Rock, Paul Ashford. Back: Tony Bogan, Pat McCarthy.

to be continued...

BRAY - DID YOU KNOW...?

County Wicklow · Ireland

braydidyouknow@gmail.com

The 'Miami Showband Massacre' (Part II of III)

The Miami Showband in 1973: Front: Martin Branigan, Paul Ashford. Standing: Fran O'Toole, Clem Quinn, Brian McCoy, Des Lee, Billy Mac

In 1972, the group had another major change, when Dickie Rock left to front his own band, and was replaced in the Miami Showband at first by brothers Frankie and Johnny Simon and then, briefly, by Billy Mac (born Billy MacDonald). Following the sacking of Mick Roche (Billy Mac's replacement) in 1974, Fran O'Toole fronted the band, Fran was from Bray, Co. Wicklow and the group was often billed as Fran O'Toole and the Miami. The album *Miami Country* was released in 1973. Line-up changes continued, and by 1975 the last remaining member of the original line-up, Clem Quinn, had left. The group then comprised Des Lee, Brian McCoy, Tony Geraghty, Fran O'Toole, Steve Travers and Ray Millar.

In 1975, when returning from a performance in County Down, Northern Ireland, three members of the band, Fran O'Toole, Tony Geraghty, and Brian McCoy, were killed in what became known as the "Miami Showband Massacre". The Miami Showband killings was a paramilitary attack at Buskhill in County Down, in the early morning of 31 July 1975. It left five people dead at the hands of Ulster Volunteer Force (UVF) gunmen, including three members of The Miami Showband. The band, had been travelling home to Dublin after a performance in The Castle Ballroom in Banbridge, County Down. The band's minibus was stopped at a bogus military checkpoint seven miles (11 km) north of Newry. Gunmen, dressed in British Army uniforms, ordered them out of their van and to line-up by the roadside. Although at least four of the gunmen were members of the British Army's Ulster Defence Regiment (UDR), all were members of the UVF, a loyalist paramilitary group. While two of the gunmen were hiding a time bomb on the minibus, it exploded prematurely and killed them. The remaining gunmen opened fire on the band members, killing three and wounding two. Two UDR soldiers and one former soldier were found guilty of murder and received life sentences; they were released in 1998.

Fran O'Toole was from Bray.

to be continued...

Above: Two photos taken the next day at the scene of the massacre.

© Bray - Did You Know 2012

70

BRAY – DID YOU KNOW...?

County Wicklow · Ireland

braydidyouknow@gmail.com

The 'Miami Showband Massacre' (Part III of III)

After the killings, the Miami Showband regrouped and continued to perform. Des Lee fronted the band until leaving in 1978, later moving to South Africa. The group remained active until 1982, led by Charlie Chapman. On 1 August, 2005, at Vicar Street in Dublin, Des Lee, Stephen Travers and Ray Millar and Johnny Fean (Horslips), Gerry Brown (brother of Dana) and Barry Woods (ex-Newmen and Real McCoy) reformed The Miami for what was described by the late great impresario Jim Aiken as "The Greatest Showband Concert Ever Staged".

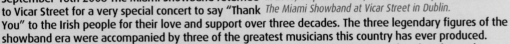

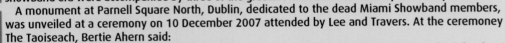

It was that very concert that started the ball rolling toward a full-blown countrywide reunion tour. On September 16th 2008 The Miami Showband returned to Vicar Street for a very special concert to say "Thank You" to the Irish people for their love and support over three decades. The three legendary figures of the showband era were accompanied by three of the greatest musicians this country has ever produced.

In 2005, Stephen Travers, Des Lee and Ray Millar reformed The Miami Showband at Vicar Street in Dublin.

A monument at Parnell Square North, Dublin, dedicated to the dead Miami Showband members, was unveiled at a ceremony on 10 December 2007 attended by Lee and Travers. At the ceremoney The Taoiseach, Bertie Ahern said:

"*Their murder was an atrocity which had such a profound impact on everyone on this island. It is remembered with sadness to this very day....We remember the affection in which they were held by people the length and breadth of Ireland. Their popularity crossed all boundaries and all traditions. They simply wanted to entertain everyone who had a love of music. At a dark time, they were a shining light for so many.*"

The music world lost three talented musicians and Ireland lost three more young men to the Troubles that faithful night back in 1975. So let us never forget those three talented boys, Fran O'Toole, Tony Geraghty and Brian McCoy.

In 2007 The Miami Showband Memorial was unveiled by the then Taoiseach Bertie Ahern.

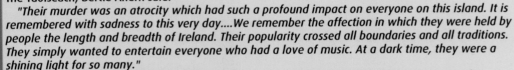

© Bray - Did You Know 2012

71

Fran O'Toole
of
The Miami
Showband

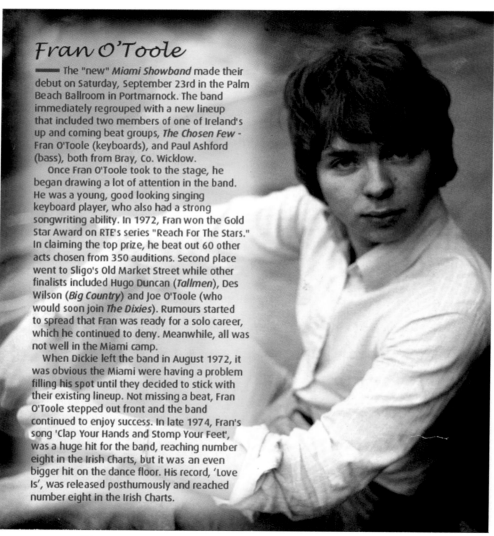

Fran O'Toole

—— The "new" *Miami Showband* made their debut on Saturday, September 23rd in the Palm Beach Ballroom in Portmarnock. The band immediately regrouped with a new lineup that included two members of one of Ireland's up and coming beat groups, *The Chosen Few* - Fran O'Toole (keyboards), and Paul Ashford (bass), both from Bray, Co. Wicklow.

Once Fran O'Toole took to the stage, he began drawing a lot of attention in the band. He was a young, good looking singing keyboard player, who also had a strong songwriting ability. In 1972, Fran won the Gold Star Award on RTE's series "Reach For The Stars." In claiming the top prize, he beat out 60 other acts chosen from 350 auditions. Second place went to Sligo's Old Market Street while other finalists included Hugo Duncan (*Tallmen*), Des Wilson (*Big Country*) and Joe O'Toole (who would soon join *The Dixies*). Rumours started to spread that Fran was ready for a solo career, which he continued to deny. Meanwhile, all was not well in the Miami camp.

When Dickie left the band in August 1972, it was obvious the Miami were having a problem filling his spot until they decided to stick with their existing lineup. Not missing a beat, Fran O'Toole stepped out front and the band continued to enjoy success. In late 1974, Fran's song 'Clap Your Hands and Stomp Your Feet', was a huge hit for the band, reaching number eight in the Irish Charts, but it was an even bigger hit on the dance floor. His record, 'Love Is', was released posthumously and reached number eight in the Irish Charts.

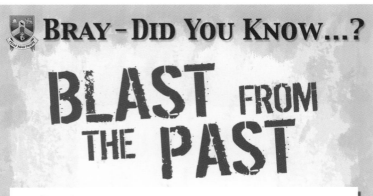

BRAY - DID YOU KNOW...?

BLAST FROM THE PAST

ST. ANNES R. C. CHURCH SHANKILL CO. DUBLIN

Shankill, Co. Dublin 1952.

An excellent photo taken of St. Anne's Church and the Shanganagh Road (right) from the railway bridge. The village of Shankill – known as *Tillystown* (after Benjamin Tilly) until the turn of the 19th Century – now has a population of just over 13,000 and is situated only 3.22 kilometers North of Bray.

BRAY DID YOU KNOW?

braydidyouknow@gmail.com

© Bray - Did You Know 2012

Shankill

A recent photo of St. Anne's Church taken from the same position.

The Freeman's Journal

★★★★★ No. 25622   Dublin, Ireland. | 3d. | VARIOUS STORIES

Fate of a Jailbreaker

24th April, 1800.

We hear from Wicklow, a man was convicted at the assizes there for breaking out of jail, and received sentence to be hanged. The unhappy man was first charged with felony, and made his escape, but being retaken was tried and acquitted, and conseqently imagined himself secure; however, he was tried again for breaking the jail, and to his great surprise was condemned to be hanged.

The use of the Knife

Bray – 1st June, 1864.

On Saturday night at about 11 o'clock, a man named John Gaffney, of violent temper, and while under the influence of liquor, had a quarrel with his wife, whom he pursued through the streets of the town, until she took refuge in the home of John Hall, of Maine Street.

On Gaffney arriving at the house he knocked violently at the door, which was opened by the owner, who remonstrated with Gaffney on his conduct, which only excited him the more, and he drew a knife from his pocket and stabbed Hall in the hip; the latter immediately seized him, and with the help of another person passing at the time, secured him until the police arrived, who took him into custody.

He is to be brought up at the next petty sessions in the town.

Poddle-hole Jack's Return

3rd July, 1776.

John Burk, alias Poddle-hole Jack, transported some years ago from Wicklow, has returned to the great terror of the inhabitants of Dorset St., it is hoped, the magistrates will be assidious in having this villain secured, that the public may not be injured by so atrocious an offender.

Effigy Burned

11th, June, 1869..

This evening about ten o'clock Judge Keogh's effigy was burned here [Bray] in presence of a very large crowd, chiefly composed of the working classes. The effigy did great credit to the executors. It was encased in a large black gown, with the word "Kehoe" in large white letters on it. Amidst great applause the effigy was fired, when the crowd increased threefold, and the local band arrived on the ground. The people dispersed peaceably and orderly, and the police arrived and held an inquest on the remains.

The Recluse of Little Sugarloaf *(Part I of II)*

One of the most extraordinary characters that have appeared in public for a long time is Edward Toole, the recluse of the Lesser Sugarloaf, near Bray, Co. Wicklow. A simple larceny was the means of revealing a series of wholesale plunders, and of making Edward Toole famous. He was charged by one of the local constabulary with having been found stealing turnips in a field belonging to Mr. Kingsmill [whom after, Kingsmill Road in Bray was named] of Novara. The prisoner was searched, and in one of the legs of his trousers was found a massive gold hunting watch, worth at least thirty guineas.

For a considerable time the constabulary were much embarrassed by the reports which came to the Bray station announcing the plunder of all kinds of property from places where it was supposed to have been most secure. Night after night policemen kept close eyes on suspected persons, but to no avail – the reports still poured in. The gold watch in Edward Toole's possession excited the suspicions of Head Constable Mercer, who searched Toole's little cabin on the Sugarloaf. This has more in common with the shanty or wigwam of an Indian than an ordinary dwelling. It is situated in a lonely and romantic place on the slopes of the Lesser Sugarloaf Mountain, it is thatched and bears no chimney on its gables. Far removed from the public thoroughfare, or from the inquisitive eye of the tourist, its inhabitant practised those 'black mail levyings' on his neighbours which made Rob Roy in other times so famous.

to be continued...

The Recluse of Little Sugarloaf *(Part II of II)*

What a sight met the Head Constable's eyes. Cautious frugality was everywhere to be seen, and everything that the recluse could demand in a place far removed from shops was arranged with the greatest order – onions, apples, wheat, turf, potatoes, garden rakes, bill-hooks, pruning knives, marquees, tents, spades, shovels, rabbit traps, ropes, fisherman's nets, and a tub full of strong pickle, from which a large quantity of good mutton had been recently removed. Head Constable Mercer opened two large trunks containing towels, stockings, handkerchiefs, gowns, children's frocks, books, a large quantity of salt for saving mutton, about seven pounds of suet, a candle mould and a Bible. However, the greatest object of interest in Toole's museum was a most ingenious rope ladder. With this portable contrivance any garden wall or outhouse could be easily scaled. Among the stolen articles was a footbath belonging to Judge Keogh, one of the marquees was identified by Mr. Blackburn as his.

Note: A Francis Blackburne sentenced the Young Irelanders, while Judge Keogh of Bushy Park near Bray, sentenced the Fenian leadership to penal servitude in 1865.

Before Bray Court

Edward Toole was brought up on remand from Wicklow jail, charged with the illegal possession of linen and clothing, two silver spoons and a gold watch. This case excited considerable interest. Toole, is, according to the description in the *Police Gazette*, or *Hue and Cry*, a native of Bray, 40 years old, five feet eight inches tall, of light make, sallow, long face, small eyes, long nose, bald, with whiskers and moustache 'painted Black'. He resided in Dublin in 1848, and has travelled through England, Scotland, France, and America.

On being called on for his defence, Toole complained in strong language of 'low scurrilous newspapers publishing defamatory libels on him, to please the low dross of the neighbourhood of Bray – counter-jumpers and the dross of society' – he concluded with a distinct denial of 'the guilt of any crime'.

Freeman's Journal, 23rd October and 5th November 1861.

Bray Courthouse and Royal Hotel

BRAY - DID YOU KNOW...?

County Wicklow · Ireland

braydidyouknow@gmail.com

Bray's Old Shops

A Quinsborough Road photo c. 1975. Behind is the Lido Cafe & Restaurant, the building is now demolished. Next to that is Waldron & Sons and then at No. 10 is Byrne's. The two children are Geraldine and Padraig O'Toole.

The Two Euro shop is here today, and the Bray Sports Centre was also located here. But in the 1950s Scottey's was the place for Ladies clothing.

Looking for something?
If you're looking for good value in coats, frocks, blouses, underwear or nylons, then the place you're looking for is Scottey's of 21 Main Street . . . the shop for smartness and low prices.

Scottey's

21, MAIN STREET, BRAY.

Caprani's pork butchers was one of Bray's landmark businesses that had been trading for nearly 70 years on Bray's Main street. Caprani's closed its doors for the last time on 9 Feb. 2002.

Hayes' Butchers on the Florence Road is one of the longest established butchers in Bray. This photo was taken around Christmas as the wide variety of turkeys in their window display proves.

:: THE ::
HOME & COLONIAL
STORES LTD.
5 Quinsboro' Road
BRANCHES THROUGHOUT THE FREE STATE

HIGH-CLASS
Groceries and Provisions
H. & C. for Quality and Value!

The Home & Colonial was situated on the Quinsborough Road and was always a favourite place to shop for the people of Bray. The Bray People office is located here now.

BRAY - DID YOU KNOW...?

County Wicklow · Ireland

braydidyouknow@gmail.com

POSTCARDS FROM BRAY

A railway company postcard from c. 1898 looking north along Bray beach and promenade.
The white building (left) is the Bray Head Hotel, which was one of the first large hotels in Bray.

The Kish Lighthouse (Part I of II)

The Kish lighthouse may not be in Bray, but it has been there since the early 1800s and it is a part of the view when one gazes out at the horizon from Bray's promenade.

In August 1810, it was decided by the Corporation for preserving and Improving the Port of Dublin (the Ballast Board), later to become the Commissioners of Irish Lights, that it would be possible to maintain a floating light on the Kish Bank. The following year they purchased the Galliot Veronia Gesina of 103 tons, engaged a crew and fitted out the vessels as a floating light. The light was first exhibited on 16th November 1811. In foggy weather a gong was sounded but when the Holyhead Packet was expected an 18 pounder gun was fired.

In 1842 an attempt was made to erect a lighthouse on the Kish Bank using screw piles invented by Alexander Mitchell but the piles were destroyed in November of that year by a severe gale and the project was abandoned. In November 1949 a radiobeacon was put into operation on this station and five years later the first of the all electric lightvessels Gannet was placed on the station. A racon was fitted in 1960. From 1946 the fog signal which gave one report every 2½ minutes was accompanied by a brilliant flash in hours of darkness during foggy weather.

In 1954 the colour of the lightvessel was changed from black to red and the character changed to Fl W 60 seconds with a flash length of 0.4 seconds. In 1956 the character changed to a double white flash every 30 seconds. From November 1957 the light was exhibited in daylight during conditions of poor visibility. In 1962 the daymarks on the Kish were discontinued.

Following the International Lighthouse Conference held at Washington in 1960, the Commissioners became interested in the possibility of using a platform similar to those used as oil rigs for lighthouse purposes and they asked nine engineering firms to submit design tenders for such a lighthouse. Various designs were submitted and that of Messrs Christiani & Nielsen Ltd was eventually selected. This design was not for a steel platform like an oil rig but a concrete lighthouse designed to last for at least 75 years, on the lines of similar lighthouses in Sweden. Model tests were carried out in Copenhagen and in Holland to check the design, stability, and foundation bearing pressures using samples of sand from the Kish Bank, and under maximum anticipated wave conditions. In order to meet Irish Sea weather conditions the structure had to be more than twice as big as the largest of similar lighthouses built by the Swedish Board of Shipping and Navigation...

to be continued...

Top: The Kish as it is today. Right: Construction of the new Kish lighthouse at Dún Laoghaire in November 1964.

The Kish Lighthouse (Part II of II)

Test borings had been made during 1961 and also a seismic survey which indicated that there is about 300 feet of sand at the site of the proposed lighthouse on the Kish Bank. It was planned to build the lighthouse of reinforced concrete in the form of a circular caisson inside which would be a tower which, when floated to its site, would be telescoped up to its full height. The tower would contain the lantern, keepers' quarters, storage, generator, radio equipment, etc.

Construction work commenced at Dun Laoghaire in July 1963. A site was prepared in the inner harbour and this was surrounded by a wall of sheet piling where the base was to be constructed. Unfortunately when the base was floated off the site it grounded unevenly and this caused damage which was increased when, during a storm in December 1963, the caisson was sunk. When it was raised a thick concrete slab was used on the top - to use it as a buoyant base on which to build a new structure.

The construction of the lighthouse was soon under way again, the bottom portion being built as a caisson and three concentric walls of varying heights, the greatest being 91 feet. These walls, interlocked by twelve radial walls forming sections which were flooded as required during the sinking operation. The tower is a self contained unit of twelve floors built within the caisson. It is 100 feet high and surmounted by a 32 feet diameter helicopter landing platform which is surrounded by a safety net.

In November 1964 the caisson was towed to St. Michael's wharf where the construction was almost completed and on the evening of 29th June 1965, it was towed out of Dun Laoghaire Harbour to the Kish Bank and later sunk on a level platform of stones which had previously been prepared by divers and buoyed by the Irish Lights Tenders. The operation of raising the tower was completed on 27 July 1965. This was done by flooding the lower caisson with water causing the tower to float up some 54 feet 6 inches and the final lift was achieved by jacks and pre-stressing cables built into the lip of the base - ensuring the tower was kept vertical. The water was then pumped out and replaced by 18,000 tons of sand and topped with concrete. The tower is white with a red band. On 9 November 1965 the Kish Lightvessel was withdrawn and replaced by Kish Lighthouse whose equipment includes a catoptric lantern giving a two million candlepower beam every 30 seconds giving a range of 27 nautical miles which can be increased to three million in fog; a racon or radar responding beacon, established in 1968, which shows on the radar screens of vessels as an unmistakable and identifiable blip; and a radiobeacon. Stores can be landed by a hydraulically controlled crane mounted on rails.

On 7 April 1992 the lighthouse was converted to automatic operation and the Keepers were withdrawn from the station. The radiobeacon was discontinued at this time. The station is in the care of an Attendant and the aids to navigation are also monitored via a telemetry link from CIL Dun Laoghaire. On 11 January 2011, as a result of an aids to navigation review, the fog signal at Kish Lighthouse was permanently discontinued, and will sound no more.

Above: The Kish lighthouse being towed out of Dun Laoghaire harbour to the Kish Bank.

LORETO CONVENT *(Part I of IV)*

Called the 'Institute of the Blessed Virgin Mary', or better known as the Loreto Sisters, was the first religious order to come to Bray. Their first small private house on the outskirts of Dublin was named "Loreto" after the famous shrine of the same name in Italy. From that day they were properly called after the name of their first modest domicile and eventually accepted it themselves.

The convent they purchased in Bray was originally called 'Bray Head House' and was owned by the Putland family for fifty years. At the end of a long avenue surrounded by fields where cattle grazed stood the main residence – later called Sans Souci – and it is told that there was a family quarrel. After several attempts to restore peace had failed they decided to sell out and gave instructions to his solicitor and named a reserve. This figure was offered by the representatives of the Loreto nuns (under the guidance of Mother Teresa Ball) and accepted by the solicitor, both unaware of the owner's real intentions. After many months, the bargain was eventually sealed. Mr. Putland then built an equally fine mansion on another part of his estate in Bray, quite close

An old photo of Loreto and the cast-iron conservatory.

at hand – which he also named 'Bray Head House', but it too passed from the family, except for a couple of intervening tenants, to the Presentation Brothers where they presently run a well-known school.

The nuns settled into their new convent, which was dedicated to St. Columba – Mother Conception Lopez being the first appointed Superior – on its own grounds of 78 acres, 100ft above sea level, which opened on January 7, 1851. An extract from a local newspaper dated 2nd January, 1851 stated: *'Bray Head House – Some months since the mansion and beautiful grounds at Bray Head were purchased for the religious order of Loretto, whose chief establishment is at Rathfarnham. The mansion has since been fitted up and the grounds arranged in the most tasteful manner, for a convent & school, which is to be opened on the 7th of this month, for the reception of boarders and day-pupils, under the superintendence of one of the ladies of the order, eminently qualified for so important a position.'*

Above: Main door of Loreto Convent in 1932 and above right: Mother Teresa Ball.

to be continued...

BRAY - DID YOU KNOW...?

County Wicklow · Ireland

braydidyouknow@gmail.com

PAST PUPILS GALLERY 1

Top Left: The Senior Orchestra 1908; Top Right: Holy Communion at Loreto Convent 1949; Bottom Left: Confirmation Class of 1957; Bottom Right: Leaving Cert Class of 1994.

LORETO CONVENT *(Part II of IV)*

The house was described as 'a chaste and elegant structure of the Tuscan order'. Beside the main house a conservatory was erected by the Putland family in 1834 at a cost of £5,000. It is still there today, but in a rather dilapidated state. The nuns opened a private boarding school in 1850 with seventy to ninety pupils and then added a secondary day school where all subjects were taught up to university entrance examination level. With a community of forty nuns, they expanded their activities rapidly and soon added a primary school. Additional extensive additions were made to the main building in 1862. The present national school for girls was built for 300 pupils, but the numbers increased so much that the nuns had to purchase the "Drummond Institute" in 1944, now called St. Patrick's Primary School. This building had been through a number of changes, starting as the Meath Industrial School, then the Duke of Connaught Hospital, and the Royal Drummond Institution for orphan girls of deceased soldiers.

Aerial photo c. 1960 showing Loreto Convent on the right and the burial vault is in the trees behind St. Patrick's School.

St. Laurence's High Class Intermediate School was an attempt to supply Second Education for boys, but it only lasted until September 1906 after which there was no facility for the Catholic boys of Bray to receive post-primary education in the town until 1920, when the Presentation Brothers acquired Mr. Putland's residence at Bray Head and opened a school there.

During both World Wars, Loreto Convent School thrived, accommodating extra students from England, France and Spain. In the 60s the move was toward 'free education' giving 'equality of educational opportunity to all'. In September 1967 the 'Free Education Act' was introduced and Loreto Bray decided to join this scheme. The next four decades would see big changes at Loreto Convent.

to be continued...

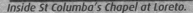

Inside St Columba's Chapel at Loreto.

BRAY - DID YOU KNOW...?

County Wicklow · Ireland

braydidyouknow@gmail.com

PAST PUPILS GALLERY 2

Top left: Taken on the steps of the school in 1882, this is the earliest pictorial record in existance of Loreto, Bray; Top right: Holy Communion Group 1965; Bottom Left: Loreto girls having fun in 1983 (for more details visit 'Loreto Convent Bray' on facebook); Bottom right: Class of 1978.

LORETO CONVENT *(Part III of IV)*

The new wing (St. Joseph's) was begun in 1970, it comprising of a reception area, an administrative block, a staff room (extended in 1986/1987), nine classrooms, a geography room, two science laboratories, a sewing room, a kitchen and an art room. It was ready for occupation by September 1971.

In 1978 the Concert Hall was connected to St. Joseph's, adding three more classrooms and converting the St. Francis Xavier's dormitory above the Concert Hall to a further three classrooms.

However, in June 1979 the boarding school finally closed, after a careful phasing out. The all weather pitch and hard tennis courts were added. In 1989 St. Columba's Chapel was deconsecrated. A locker room in St. Joseph's was converted into a new prayer room and a second locker room turned into a music room in 1993. In 1995/1996 'Harmony Heights', previously boarder's bedrooms, was converted into a spacious computer suite and a canteen was provided in St. Columba's. The year 1999 saw the Mary Ward building opened comprising of an oratory, a stage with large auditorium, a language laboratory, art room, three science laboratories, a home economics room, music room, business room, teacher's work room and a small kitchenette.

The astro-turf pitch was constructed in 2000 and changing rooms were added on in 2003. The sports hall, with gym suite was completed in 2009.

to be continued...

Above: A Valentine postcard from c.1905; Top right: The Parlour at Loreto and the Sports Field (above) c. 1910.

PAST PUPILS GALLERY 3

Clockwise from below left: The Class of 1980; School group at Grotto c. 1959; Students in the 80s (for details visit 'Loreto Convent Bray' on facebook). Loreto Girls outside the Church of the Most Holy Redeemer.

Photo includes: Rosaleen Walsh, Patricia McDonnell, Detta Flood, Joan Maher, Collette and Nuala Scullion, Euneen Doherty, Una Maguire, Dympna & Terry Corcoran, Deirdre McDonnell, Mary Watson, Marie O'Grady, Una Pender, Catriona Kelly, Ann Doyne, Joan Cleary, Rosemary O'Rourke, Joan Doyne, Betty Kickham, Linda Hutton, Marie McDonnell, Jackie Sweeney, Maeve Maguire, Nuala Cotter, Betty Thompson, Maura Donegan, Marie Callis, Patricia Mullen and Ann Gordon.

LORETO CONVENT *(Part IV of IV)*

Almost covered in dense growth, hidden from view at the rear of Sans Souci is the old nuns graveyard and vault, which is also a final resting place for many nuns on the grounds of Loreto Convent. The vault stands on a hill above a grotto (recently removed) inspired by the Grotto of Lourdes, France. All but one of its late residents were ladies of the cloth, with the exception of a Loreto girl believed to have drowned while holidaying in Spain. The girl was supposedly a friend of the daughter of a member of the Spanish nobility who had been a pupil at the school.

But locals believed that in the crypt-style circular wall, the nuns were buried standing upright. The rumours that some of the gravestones had a rat engraved on the surface, supposedly meaning that the headstone marked as such indicated that the nun had succumbed to the plague. But this seems to be far-fetched as the only emblem on the headstones which were visible are the cross and the 'Lamb of God'.

The entrance gates on the Vevay Road, which were surmounted by a small cross, are gone now, it is now the entrance to the Vevay Crescent housing estate. With the continued growth of Bray, pressure on land close to the town centre has finally affected the grounds of the Loreto Convent; houses now occupy the walled garden and a large area at the southern end, while St Thomas's Community College has been built within the northern perimeter.

The old gateway leading from the avenue to the grotto and vault.

Top: The vault on the hill which contains the remains of some of the Loreto Sisters; Above left: Inside the vault is overgrown; Inset: an emblem of the Lamb on the Cross, which was probably mistaken by many as a rat; Above right: the conservatory (built 1834) is in a dilapidated state.

BRAY - DID YOU KNOW...?

County Wicklow · Ireland

braydidyouknow@gmail.com

PAST PUPILS GALLERY 4

Top left: Mother Margaret Mary with the Leaving Cert Class of 1950;
Top right: A 2003 re-union of the Class of '83;
Below left: Loreto girls on an outing during the 1980s (for details visit 'Loreto Convent Bray' on facebook);
Below centre: Loreto National School 1938 / '39, See details below.

Photo includes: Jackie Cranley, Phyllis McDnnell, J. McGuinness, Patrick Hipwell, Bridie Murphy, Betty Murphy, Kathleen Brien, Eileen Brien, Essie Murray and Bridie Hyland.

BRAY - DID YOU KNOW...?

County Wicklow · Ireland

braydidyouknow@gmail.com

Top right: Loreto girls during the 1980s (for details visit 'Loreto Convent Bray' on facebook);
Bottom left: Loreto girls at the Debutantes Ball at Killiney Castle Hotel in October, 1983 (for details visit 'Loreto Convent Bray' on facebook);
Bottom right: Loreto girls with the 'Peter Pan Collar' style in 1949;

PAST PUPILS GALLERY 5

PAST PUPILS GALLERY 6

Top left: Class of '83 enjoying the sportsday;
Top right: A reunion photo of the Class of '80;
Bottom left: Loreto School Students June 1958;
Bottom right: The Juniors Communion day 1973.

© Bray - Did You Know 2012

King Louis XVI and the Nuns of Loreto Convent

The roads of Ireland in the first decades of the twentieth century saw a constant stream of tramps. George Finnerton came to the Vevay in the early 1930s from where, nobody knows. George was a tall, distinguished man who always carried a bundle of newspapers under his arm was well versed in all the disciplines and knew countless verses from the Bible by heart.

George's first stop when he arrived in Bray was to Loreto Convent where he was offered a little pay with all meals if he would agree to hoe and rake a little of the avenue each day, a deal that suited him. George took up residence in the burial vaults behind the convent, where the Foundress and first Sisters are interred.

Some of the locals looked out for George and, on one such occasion, in the depts of winter, he was visited by two local men, who groped their way up the embankment guided by the storm lantern that George used to read by in the burial vault, he was asked whether he was afraid of sleeping with the dead, he answered... ' *Not at all, the little Sisters are great company*!'

One night, George was given a bundle. It was a complete costume of Louis XVI, King of France. '*Thank you gentlemen*' was George's reply, *I will be honoured to wear it*." Next morning, in full costume, George stepped out to rake the avenue. It was custom at that time for the nuns to walk the grounds reading their prayerbooks when one young novice, thinking that she was looking at a ghost from times past, fainted.
The news soon reached the reverend mother who sent for the police, who found George raking away, un-aware of the commotion he had just caused!
One morning, soon after, George was nowhere to be found. Who he was or where he went was never to be told.

From Griffin & Sons to Anvil

Even at the turn of the 19th century, Bray had some wonderful shops and businesses, and some of these were right in the heart of the Main Street. Mrs. Cullen ran her dairy business at no. 22. At the time no. 23 was vacant, but Mr. *J.E. Griffin & Sons* had a busy ironmonger business in no. 24.

By 1910 Mrs. Cullen was now running a grocers shop and Mr. Griffin's was soon to expand and over the next few years took over Mrs. Cullen's premises next door at no. 22. He was now not only running his ironmonger's but his general merchant's business was booming. His well-stocked shop sold furniture, china, glassware and seed etc and was a very popular business for years in Bray town. The hardware company *Murdoch's* took over the premises in the 1940s and ran their very successful hardware and builders providers services from here for decades until *Anvil's* took over in 1971, are still going strong today.

Top right: Griffin & Sons as it was c.1914; Bottom right: The Main Street c.1964 with Murdoch's centre picture; Right: No's. 22 - 24 as Anvil today.

BRAY – DID YOU KNOW...?

County Wicklow · Ireland

braydidyouknow@gmail.com

The Quinsborough Road (Part I of II)

A new road, which would lead from the Main Street of Bray town to the sea was planned, laid out and opened by the Dublin and Wicklow Railway Company to coincide with the opening of the railway in 1854, although there is some question as to when exactly it was fully opened up at the western end.

Named the Quinsborough Road, after Mr. John Quin, who supplied the land from his hotel on the Main Street to the railway station. It was Quin's agreement with the Dublin & Wicklow Railway Co. that determined the siting of the railway station close to the seaward end of *Quin's Walk* – a private pathway, which led from the rear of Quin's Hotel (now the Royal Hotel) to the seafront - part of which is now Duncairn Terrace. The same agreement stipulated that the railway company would pay for the new 'forty-foot' road (which the road was sometimes called back then) running parallel to *Quin's Walk* from the Main Street across the

QUINSBOROUGH ROAD, BRAY

level crossing to the seafront. Quinsborough Road became the main artery between the old Bray and the new, breaking into the Main Street across the old *Turks Head* public house - which had to be demolished - south of Quin's Hotel and offering an enticing vista towards the sea from the heart of the old town.

After the railway had arrived in 1854, a boom period in 19th century Bray lasted just a few years until around 1860. From about 1858, the development of suburban houses and hotels expanded rapidly, but the boom was waning by 1863. Virtually all the best Victorian developments in Bray stem from this short period, including Christ Church in 1863, Breslin's Royal Marine Hotel - built slightly earlier in 1855, and the International Hotel opened in 1862. Together they were the only large hotels (apart from the older Quin's Hotel) until the turn of the century.

to be continued...

Left: Looking west along the Quinsborough c. 1890;
Top right: Main Street, Quinsborough Road and Herbert Road junction in 1895.

© Bray – Did You Know 2012

93

BRAY – DID YOU KNOW...?

County Wicklow · Ireland

braydidyouknow@gmail.com

The Quinsborough Road (Part II of II)

There were also numerous terraces built. Dargan Terrace (now Duncairn Terrace) was built in 1859 by William Dargan, and in 1860-61 came the Prince of Wales Terrace. Goldsmith Terrace (below right) was originally a uniform row of twelve houses, built in 1863 – one of which would become the Imperial Hotel - and of course there was the Prince of Wales Terrace and the Turkish Baths – all were built to face each other across the wide street, made even more imposing by its private roadway on the northern side. Even today, after various vicissitudes, this is the most imposing stretch of road in Bray.

West of Goldsmith Terrace and the Turkish Baths (now the Boulevard Centre), the road has a different, less impressive character and the façades have fewer pretensions to grandeur; it might be suggested that the new houses and shops here were built after the first hopes for a booming resort had faded.

The main impetus for this development came from a small group of property owners, financiers and contractors. John Quin - the younger - received possession of his father's lands, stretching from the Main Street to the sea, in 1852. He sold the station area to the railway and assigned thirteen acres to William Dargan in 1858, including much of the site of Quinsborough Road, which became the town's premier shopping and residential area. Certainly there was a difference in the character of the pre-existing property parcels nearer the sea, which was virtual virgin territory, and the more fragmented parcels in the west that had formerly included the backyards of properties in the main street. Other building leases followed with covenants to build to specified standards. One can see in these leases the landlord enforcing his own use zoning, density zoning and services provision, as a planning authority would today.

Bóthar Bhaile Ui Chuínn
QUINNSBOROUGH ROAD

Top: Looking east along the Quinsboro' Road c. 1910.
Right: The fine houses of Goldsmith Terrace built by Dargan. Note the 'Imperial Hotel', which is the white building in the centre of the terrace - photo c. 1922.

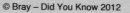

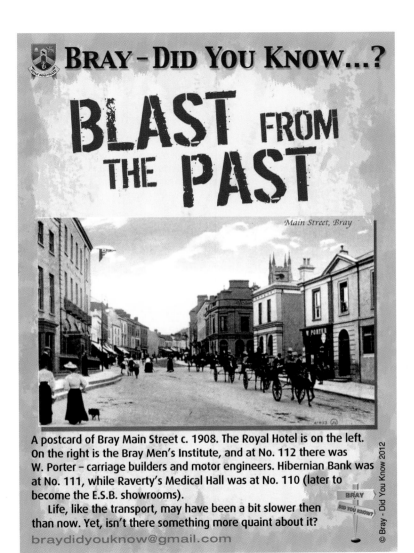

BLAST FROM THE PAST

Main Street, Bray

A postcard of Bray Main Street c. 1908. The Royal Hotel is on the left. On the right is the Bray Men's Institute, and at No. 112 there was W. Porter – carriage builders and motor engineers. Hibernian Bank was at No. 111, while Raverty's Medical Hall was at No. 110 (later to become the E.S.B. showrooms).

Life, like the transport, may have been a bit slower then than now. Yet, isn't there something more quaint about it?

braydidyouknow@gmail.com

BRAY DID YOU KNOW?

© Bray - Did You Know 2012

The Main Street

Bray Main Street c. 1880 - one of the oldest known photos of the Main Street.

Lochner's – the pork butchers (from *A Pictorial History of Bray, Co. Wicklow Vol. 6* by Henry Cairns & Owen Gallagher)

Mention the name *Lochner* in or around Bray and the first thing that will come to many minds is the fine pork butcher shops on Bray's Main Street. Lochner's were a German family who had their shops at various locations on the street over a period of more than 60 years. Their wonderful products, including puddings, sausages and chops, were a must on the shopping lists of many while shopping in Bray. But like *Caprani's* – a competitor to Charles Lochner – and many other great shops in Bray, they are no more. The following short story was written about the family businesses by Charles Lochner's grandson, Ralph Lochner, in November 2007...

My grandfather, Charles Lochner left his native town of Künzelsau (about 40 miles from Stuttgart) in Germany and moved to England around 1900. He married Marie Primmer in Bradford, Leeds in 1902. They moved to Kirkham in Lancashire where he set up business as a pork butcher and started a family. There were three boys and four girls, the eldest Herbert then Eva, Ernest, Phyllis, Freda, Eunice and the youngest Frederick. When the First World War began in 1914, all German nationals were interned and my grandfather was no exception. I'm not sure where he was interned, but on his release in 1916 he made his way to Ireland. The rest of the family followed and in 1917 he set up business as a pork butcher in 102 Main Street, Bray. The family lived over the shop – as was the custom of the time. He and the family worked hard and early in 1950 they were able to purchase a much larger premises next door, which was 101. He also acquired 98 Main Street, also as a pork butchers.

The O'Brien brothers were the main building contractors and superb craftmanship and materials were used throughout the shop at 101. The shop window shape was quite unique and was mentioned in a book about Irish shopfronts. Above the shop door was an unusual sign, it was a halfpenny (½ d - pre decimal currency) which was in common use at the time. My grandfather had the distinction of breeding and showing the first Irish Champion German Shepherd dog in, I think, 1930. Charles Lochner died in 1960 aged 85 and his wife died in 1953 aged 78. All the original members of the family are dead, my father Ernest and his wife Evellyn who had emigrated to New Zealand in 1987 was the last to die in 1996 aged 93. My mother is still alive and living in Auckland aged 91. The shop at 101 Main Street finally closed as a pork butchers on 7th April 1979.

Ralph Lochner.

Clockwise from top: The Lochner family c. 1957; Charles and Marie Lochner; Charles Lochner at his shop c. 1920; Lochner's shop at 101 Main Street.

Double Deaths at Bray Railway Station *(Part I of II)*

On Saturday February 21, 1908 the mail train from Wexford arrived in Bray Railway Station shortly after 7 p.m., and when the train had stopped the No. 2 engine was detached from the carriages and allowed to run forward for the purpose of being shunted into the sheds. At that time three tracks were opposite the platform; the furthest track from the platform was known as the 'shed rail', which ran close along by the wall and ended in a stop block. There was a carriage resting at the stop block, which would be needed later and shunted on to a Dublin bound train.

Meantime the engine, which had been detached from the carriages, was moving about. It returned to the points which would allow it to pass over the middle track and cross the main track behind the carriages to the shed. While all this engine movement was in progress, two railway men, William Needham and Timothy Doyle (who was Captain of the Wicklow Hurling team), went to the carriage at the stop block and began to pull the carriage towards the points. However, they did not inform the signalman, Michael Quail, in the South cabin of their plans.

The two men had managed to pull the carriage about 15 yards when the engine came down the track, crossed the points and due to the angle of the carriage struck it in front and drove it back with great force. Doyle and Needham were thrown to the ground and fell over part of the rail and the carriage passed over their legs, causing severe injuries to both. The carriage then hit the stop block and bounced back striking the unfortunate men a second time. Laurence Doyle, the driver of the locomotive, left the footplate after he had stopped the engine and ran to where the two injured men lay. So did Thomas Doyle, who was on duty at the Quinsborough Road level crossing.

In the presence of both men, Timothy Doyle admitted that the accident was his own fault. Station Master Roberts hurried to the scene and sent for the clergy and medical help. Dr. Monsell and Dr. Brew arrived promptly and their examinations of both men revealed that Needham's legs were very badly injured, while Doyle's were severed below the knees. He was also suffering from internal injuries.

The turntable at Bray Station (now removed) was near to where the accident happened.

to be continued...

Double Deaths at Bray Railway Station *(Part II of II)*

Needham was taken to Dublin on the 7.10 p.m. Dublin bound train whose departure had been held up. It left at 7.23 p.m. with Dr. Monsell and on arrival in Dublin Needham was taken to the Meath Hospital. Doyle was removed to Dublin by engine and van which left at 8.30 p.m. with Dr. Brew and on arrival in Dublin Doyle was also taken to the Meath Hospital.

Despite frantic efforts by the medical staff of the hospital, William Needham died at around 9 p.m. and Timothy Doyle at around 10 p.m.

Dr. Louis A. Byrne, the City Coroner, conducted an inquest on the two men at the Dublin Morgue on Monday 23 February. Mr. A.E. Bradly represented the Railway Co. Mr. Joseph Gleeson represented the Amalgamated Society of Railway Servants and relatives of the deceased, while Sgt. Slator and Constable Finneran the Police.

The jury received a full account of what had happened from an array of witnesses, and in returning a verdict of accidental death exonerated the engine driver Laurence Doyle and the signalman Michael Quail from all blame. It was emphasised that all future cases should be treated by the nearest hospital, as there was a long discussion during the inquest as to whether their lives could have been saved had they been taken to a nearer hospital.

Railway Station, Bray, Co. Wicklow. c.1905

Ray O'Donnell

Left: Bray Railway Station c. 1908; Right: A c.1905 postcard of Bray Railway Station showing the three tracks opposite the platform.

Old Court Castle (Part I of II)

There are two known versions of the origin of Old Court Castle. The first is taken from the *Dublin Penny Journal* of 1833 which states that in 1440 – during the reign of Henry VI – Old Court Castle was built by an English knight named Sir Esmond or Edmond Mulso, who obtained a grant of land there in what was then called the marshes of Co. Dublin, on condition of reducing it to a state of order and obedience to the English government. He succeeded in taking possession of the land and building the castle, which he called 'Mulso's Castle' (now Old Court Castle). But Mulso was killed afterwards in a skirmish, and the castle passed into other hands.

The other version is from Canon Digby Scott and he takes it from the 1910 *'Statute Rolls, Ireland, Henry VI.,'* and states that:

"...the castle was in the possession of the Edwards family, it looks as if a bad guess was made in identifying Old Court with the unknown, possibly never created, Mulsoescourt. And now, to try to make a better guess, I should suggest that as it is in connection with the Earl of Ormond's manor of Bree that Old Court is mentioned in the 11th year of Henry VI. In the Pembroke Estate Deeds, probably it was that illustrious family [Ormond's] which had built the castle for the defences and administration of their manor so long before, that it had already come to be called Old Court by that time."

Whichever version is correct, at least history does tell us that Mulso's Castle was owned by the Earl of Ormond at one stage.

In 1595 two failed expeditions led by Lord Deputy Russell to Glenmalure to fight against Feagh Mac Hugh O'Byrne were made from Mulso's Castle and from Bray Castle. One such expedition consisted of 1,100 men with provisions and machines for hurling stones.

to be continued...

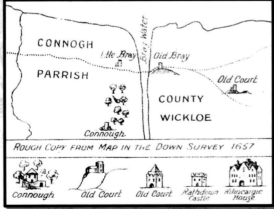

Bottom right: Rough copies of drawings from the 17th century Down Survey maps showing four castles in Bray, including Old Court;
Top left: The castle as it was in c. 1910;
Top right: Old Court Castle as it is today.

Old Court Castle *(Part II of II)*

The castle eventually passed into the possession of the Walshes of Carrickmines. Theobald or Tibbald Walsh occupied the castle in 1620, the castle was occupied by a widow, Joan Eustace by 1630.

In the 'Down Survey' (1657) it was described as "a castle repairable." After the 1661 Act of Settlement, the castle and lands were granted to Richard Edwards Esq., a Welsh gentleman and Elizabeth his wife, who held it till the latter part of the 19th century, and their memory is preserved by a very large burial enclosure at St. Paul's Churchyard (opposite the Royal hotel). But, fortunately for its preservation, the castle fell into the careful hands of the Earl of Meath.

On its south-west side, the lines of the high-pitched roof which abutted against it can still be seen, where a large wing was built against it, containing, no doubt, all the comfortable and most habitable parts of the house. The castle is drawn on a map of the 'Down Survey', with this wing attached to the square tower. The opening by which you can now enter the tower was originally an entrance from the upper floor of this wing. It has a spiral stairwell leading to the second and fourth floors. You will also notice the gateway of the courtyard, with the ruins of the two small round towers that defended it, however, only the entrance to the western tower remains.

Thankfully the ruins of Old Court castle still stand and are now situated on private property off the Vevay Road south of Bray town, and the resident of the property usually won't mind you visiting providing you ask permission first.

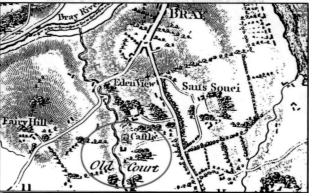

Above: A photo of the ruins of Old Court Castle; Right: A part of the 1821 William Duncan map showing Bray town and Old Court with the castle marked out in red.

Sir Stanley Cochrane of Woodbrook (Part I of II)

A remarkable sporting personality named Sir Stanley Cochrane who had served with the Dublin Fusiliers in the First World War lived on a large estate at Woodbrook, just north of the town of Bray. He rose to the level of captain of the 7th Batallion, during this time his city residence was 45 Kildare Street, which was also being used in the war effort.

The flourishing mineral water company of Cantrell and Cochrane (C&C), founded by his father, had made him a wealthy man. The company was originally founded by T.J. Cantrell for the purpose of making and distributing mineral waters and aerated sarsaparilla, together with Stanley's father, Sir Henry Cochrane Bart, who managed the Company operating out of 2,3 and 4 Nassau Place in Dublin. Under Henry's stewardship the company became extremely successful despite the stiff international competition in the industry.

Sir Stanley was a cricket enthusiast the lengths he went to for his love of the game are the stuff of legend. He had the money to indulge in patronage of the most

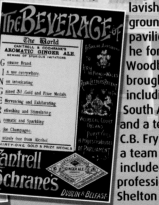

lavish kind and made a first class ground complete with an elegant pavilion overlooking it. In 1907 he formed a club known as Woodbrook Club and Ground, and brought over world class teams including the Australians, the South Africans, Indians, Yorkshire and a team captained by the great C.B. Fry. In addition he maintained a team at Woodbrook which included some eminent professionals and hired Harry Shelton to coach them before the war.

Woodbrook and its beautiful gardens are just outside Bray.

Sir Stanley Cochrane of Woodbrook (Part II of II)

Cochrane was one of the first men in Ireland to take an interest in motoring and owned a fleet of expensive cars including two Rolls Royces. During the cricket years, Cochrane was also deeply involved in music. Behind the house he built what he originally intended as an indoor cricket pitch, but later transformed it into an opera house. He was responsible for bringing over the famous Quinlan Opera Company and Nellie Melba.

The cricket weeks at Woodbrook were famous throughout Britain, as well as Ireland, but such vast expenditure could hardly be maintained indefinitely and the cricket ended in 1912. Next Sir Stanley turned his attention to golf and he had a course made on land on the far side of the railway line. So eager was the response that he decided to extend the scope by forming a club which he registered under the Clubs Act and for which there was a membership fee of four guineas per annum. Soon it became prestigious to be a member of the Woodbrook Club and when the nine hole course opened in 1921, 71 joined. The names on the original Register of Members contained a wide cross-section of Dublin's professional and business leaders. In keeping with his image as a father figure to those who were his guests, Cochrane, who maintained a city house in Kildare Street, would transfer his large staff from there to Woodbrook at weekends to provide a lavish lunch, for the modest sum of 2/6.

Above: The cricket pitch was in front of the pavilion (centre building) beside the clubhouse. Below left: The gardens at Woodbrook looking west from the house.

While in New York in 1923 he travelled to Pinehurst Golf Club accompanied by Grantland Rice and Parker of the American Golfers' Association to

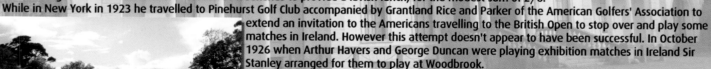

extend an invitation to the Americans travelling to the British Open to stop over and play some matches in Ireland. However this attempt doesn't appear to have been successful. In October 1926 when Arthur Havers and George Duncan were playing exhibition matches in Ireland Sir Stanley arranged for them to play at Woodbrook.

In the following years he decided to move to England and his involvement in Irish golf tapered off, but with the first Irish Open Championship arranged for 1927 he had set a foundation for Irish professionals being able to compete at a higher standard. Sir Stanley died on the 23 October 1949, but Cantrell and Cochrane would continue to sponsor professional golf and Woodbrook, the club he founded, would play host to many of the major events during the late fifties, sixties and early seventies, and would also host the Irish Open in 1975 after a twenty-one year absence from the circuit (1954-1974).

BRAY - DID YOU KNOW...?

County Wicklow · Ireland

braydidyouknow@gmail.com

POSTCARDS FROM BRAY

Aerial Chair Lift to Eagle's Nest, Bray, Co. Wicklow, Ireland.

Colour Photo by John Hinde, F.R.P.S.

The Aerial Chair Lifts on Bray Head were a major tourist attraction in Bray from the 50s to the 70s.

© Bray - Did You Know 2012

BRAY – DID YOU KNOW...?

County Wicklow · Ireland

braydidyouknow@gmail.com

BRAY BRIDGE

A very steep four-arched bridge was constructed over the Dargle River in 1666, which replaced the ford that was used at least since Anglo-Norman times. But during a raging storm in 1741, the bridge collapsed and was washed away. Within the same year, another four-arched bridge was built, and this stood until it was replaced by the present Bray Bridge, which was built by David Edge, who usually dined at the nearby Quin's Hotel in the evenings.

The bridge was officially opened on the 11th September, 1856 by Mrs. Mason of the Anchor Tavern, Bray and Mrs. Butler of Loughlinstown; they being the first to cross the water were heartily cheered by all the men on the work, every person present, who they liberally entertained that evening in celebration.

Clockwise from right: Inscription stone on the east side of the bridge; The bridge today - looking from the west side; The present Bray Bridge c.1890 - the arch on the right was used for watering horses; A painting of the Dargle River and Bray Bridge by Samuel F. Brocas c.1800 (Courtesy of Cyril Dunne); The four-arched bridge over the Dargle painted in 1847 (Bartlett), this bridge replaced the one destroyed in 1741.

BRAY - DID YOU KNOW...?

County Wicklow · Ireland

braydidyouknow@gmail.com

MADE IN BRAY

ARDMORE STUDIOS IRELAND

Michael Collins

Neil Jordan's depiction of the controversial life and death of Michael Collins, the 'Lion of Ireland', who led the IRA against British rule and founded the Irish Free State (Eire) in 1921. This 1996 blockbuster stars Liam Neeson, Aidan Quinn and Julia Roberts and was directed by Neil Jordan.

DID YOU KNOW...

• The Carlisle Grounds (home to Bray Wanderers F.C.) substituted for 1920s Croke Park massacre in Dublin, at a cost of approx IR£1 million to renovate the ground accordingly?

• Liam Neeson was 43 years old when this movie was made. The real-life Michael Collins was 31 years old when he died?

• Tom Cruise was offered the 'Jonathan Rhys-Meyers' cameo of the Assassin?

• The final piece of score by Elliot Goldenthal in the film, "Funeral/Coda," is actually Goldenthal's rejected finale for *Heat*, which director Michael Mann replaced with an existing Moby piece.

BRAY – DID YOU KNOW...?

County Wicklow · Ireland

braydidyouknow@gmail.com

St Paul's School on the Herbert Road: 1904 - 1972 *(Part I of III)*

By the end of the nineteenth century a new school was planned for Herbert Road. At that time, the only primary school for Church of Ireland children in the town stood in Little Bray (then part of Co. Dublin) and was considered quite inadequate. Known as 'Bray Bridge School', it had been endowed in 1819 and was set back on the sea-side of Castle Street near the River Dargle. Its premises shared 'a neat range of buildings, erected by subscription,' with a savings' bank for the parishes of Bray, Delgany, and Powerscourt. They were later transformed into the dwellings of what is now Belton Terrace.

The Earl of Pembroke and Montgomery who owned a considerable portion of Bray land and who had given 'a free site for the new Roman Catholic Church now in course of erection', also gave the site for the new school. Notices of the intended building (1901) and its adjacent teacher's house (1904) survive, each

An illustration of St. Paul's School by its architect J.F. Fuller (1903).

signed by Archdeacon James G. Scott, the last vicar of the Established Church in Bray and local Rector from 1862 to 1910 - whose son Canon George Digby Scott wrote *The Stones of Bray* (Dublin, 1913). Technically, St Paul's was planned as two combined schools, one for boys and one for girls.

The building, designed by the famous J.F. Fuller, was a red brick building with granite dressings, intended to accommodate 100 boys, 100 girls and 60 infants. Church of Ireland members in the expanding town had earlier seen Christ Church supersede St Paul's Church as their parish's principal place of worship, St Paul's then becoming a chapel of ease.

St Paul's School was formally dedicated and opened by Archbishop Joseph Peacocke, on the afternoon of Wednesday 22 June 1904. Psalm 127 having been read, the children sang very sweetly The Meeting of the Waters and a Brighter day is Drawing Near. The first pupils were registered on the 1 October 1904, including 59 boys and 61 girls transferred from the old Bray Bridge School. The latter premises were among many in Little Bray that later were badly hit by severe flooding in 1905.

Pupils with Teachers Mr. McMillan and Mrs. Marks c.1959.

to be continued...

St. Paul's School on the Herbert Road: 1904 - 1972 *(Part II of III)*

An aerial photo c.1948 of the Herbert Road area and the school.

Mr. James Moore and his wife, both teachers in the old parochial school, moved to St. Paul's, where Mrs. Heatley also worked as the infants' teacher. In 1925, James Moore's retirement after forty years of educational service in Bray was marked by a presentation in the Parochial Hall, Bray. He told the gathering that 1,600 pupils had passed through his hands, 'and during the Great war St. Paul's School had made a fine record. One hundred and thirty old boys had joined up, and many had made the supreme sacrifice'. Among other pupils entering his school, in 1922, had been the future actor Cyril Cusack. Cyril's teacher, Miss Moore, also left in 1925, to become principal of Rathmichael School.

The Moores were succeeded at St Paul's School by Mr and Mrs Robert Maguire. Charlie Gray, who entered as a pupil in 1938, remembers that, *"Mr Maguire was a great teacher who had a terrible temper when roused. Caning took place and I have seen a pointer being broken over someone's back. I remember being in one of the senior classes when someone whispered a funny joke. I burst out laughing. Mr Maguire asked who laughed. I said nothing. He asked again and I still didn't move. I guessed he knew it was me. He jumped up and I could see the temper rising in him and he clenched his fist as he came towards me.*

As he swung at me I dropped my chin and he hit Willie Sutton instead. That made him madder and he beat me all round the room. I didn't hold it against him. It was the norm at that time."

The school was visited regularly by the Attendance Officer – a Garda Officer. "In my time", says Charlie, "it was Garda McEneney. He would come and check the roll and if you missed even one day, you had to stand up and say why that was. Threats to be sent to Daingean or Letterfrack would follow. I didn't find out until I was about 25 that Protestants couldn't be sent to any of these places as they were run by Christian Brothers."

The rear of the school during snowy weather.

to be continued...

St Paul's School on the Herbert Road: 1904 - 1972 *(Part III of III)*

In December 2008, writing for *In Touch*, the parish magazine of Christ Church, Bray, Gillian Misstear (neé Hanan) recalled St Paul's School in the 1950s, when Mr Ernie McMillan was headmaster. She recalls lists of spellings, little squared books of sums and 'the dreaded hemming' and adds, *"I remember my indignation at having to sew while the boys were allowed to go on with their sums"*. She also remembers McMillan's three canes, *"the most feared being Ginger Dick"*.

On 22 February 1971, the names of the last pupils to enter St Paul's were registered. The school was demolished in 1972. Part of the front wall of the property and the pedestrian entrance for children, with its gateway and railings and steps up from Herbert Road, survive to the left of the vehicular entrance to the present car park behind Holy Redeemer church. The clear view of Christ Church, seen in Fuller's drawing (see Pt. I), is now obstructed by Connolly Square.

The entire register books of St Paul's Male and Female National Schools, Bray, consist of just two volumes. One is marked 'cailíní' (girls) and the other 'na buachaillí' (the boys), and both run from 1904 until 1971. After that date, St Paul's was subsumed into St Andrew's National School on the Newcourt Road in Bray. In 1998, these volumes were deposited in the National Archives of Ireland by Mr Peter McCrodden, headmaster of St Andrew's, along with 49 items relating to his own national school and a few miscellaneous notes from St Paul's.

Cannon Cambell passes the school on his way to the Holy Redeemer Church.

Are you in this St Paul's School photo c. 1950?

The gateway and spot where St Paul's school once stood.

Bike Polo and the Olympics Part I of II

The Forgotten Olympian from Bray

Richard James Mecredy (1861-1924) lived at Vallombrosa, Thornhill Road, Bray, and was regarded as the 'Father of cycling and motoring in Ireland.' Between the autumn of 1883 and 2nd July 1888 Mecredy rode in 76 cycle races, winning prizes in 71 of them! Richard won the Coronation Cup Race in 1902. In 1905 he rode 302 miles in one day, changing his tyres no fewer than six times during the race. He was editor and owner of *The Irish Cyclist* and wrote books on motoring and cycling.

His Son the Olympian

Richard's eldest son, Ralph Jack Richard Mecredy, was born on 12th July 1888 and was also a keen cyclist representing Trinity College in track and field events along with taking part in two Olympic Games in 1908 and 1912. The British Olympic Council's Official Report of the Fourth Olympiad (London 1909) shows that a game of Cycle Polo was played between The Irish Bicycle Polo Association (team pictured bottom left) and Germany's Deutscher Radfahrer Bund. On the winning Irish team were Mecredy Junior and the Oswald brothers from Rathclaren in Bray.

Ireland beat Germany 3-1 in the Shepherds Bush Stadium (London). *to be continued...*

Cycle Polo on Bray Seafront

Richard James Mecredy who invented Bicycle Polo in 1891. The first game was played in Co. Wicklow between Rathclaren Rovers and Ohne Hast Cycling Club on 4 October, 1891.

BRAY - DID YOU KNOW...?

County Wicklow · Ireland

braydidyouknow@gmail.com

Bike Polo and the Olympics Part II of II

The Birth of Cycle Polo

In 1891 at the Scalp near Enniskerry, Richard James Mecredy invented the game of Cycle Polo. The first Cycle Polo match was played between *Rathclaren Rovers* and the Ohne Hast ("Without Haste') Cycling Club. By the end of the nineteeth century the game had reached Britain, France and the USA. The first international match was played between Ireland and England at Crystal Palace, which was a comfortable win for the Irish!

Other Olympians from the Bray Area

Bray has a rich history of Bray people who participated in the Olympic Games. Here we name some well known and maybe not too well known Olympic heroes:

Bertie Messitt: Marathon Runner, **Peter Crinnion:** Cycling,

Peter Doyle: Cycling, **Gary O'Toole:** Swimming,

Robin Seymour: Mountain Bike,

Mabel Hilda Harris: Tennis,

Lilian Lucy Davidson: Art Competition,

Katie Taylor (2012 Olympics) Boxing.

Pictures left to right: 1924 Paris Olympics Poster, Katie Taylor, Robin Seymour, Gary O'Toole, Bertie Messitt, Peter Doyle.

© Bray - Did You Know 2012

Mr. Wilde and the Esplanade Terrace

Walking along the esplanade today one would come across an imposing terrace of four houses called Esplanade Terrace. Dr. William Wilde (father of Oscar) built these in 1863 during the 'boom period', which lasted about seven years. Dr. William, eye and ear surgeon and antiquarian, was one of the early developers of the town and a member of the Bray Town Commission. He also owned "Elsinore" - which is now the Strand Hotel next to the Esplanade Hotel as an investment.

Dr. Wilde was knighted by Queen Victoria for his services to the Irish Census Board on which he served as medical commissioner. His social standing was soon however to suffer a setback. An alleged indiscretion in relation to a female patient led to a chain of events ending in a libel action. The young woman in question, Mary Josephine Travers, when spurned by Sir William, started a campaign of harassment against the Wilde family. She even pursued them to Bray, where Lady Wilde (author of *Ancient Legends, Mystic Charms and Superstitions of Ireland* under the pseudonym 'Spiranza') and her children had taken refuge at Esplanade Terrace. They were believed locally to have also rented 'Tower Cottage' on the corner of Strand Road and and Putland Road at one stage – probably while their other properties were let out. This led to Lady Wilde writing a letter of complaint to the young woman's father (Professor of Medical Jurisprudence at Trinity College, Dublin). Mary Travers found the letter and sued Lady Wilde for libel. She won her case but was awarded the derisory damages of one farthing. Wilde's reputation was in shreds and he more or less retired from public life.

He died in 1876 leaving his Bray houses to his son Oscar - who sold them in 1878. The latter and an estate agent, with whom the properties were listed, accepted offers from two different bidders at the same time. The bidder who was subsequently declared unsuccessful sued. Oscar won the case in Bray Court but, with all the expenses involved, there was only £3,000 left.

Top left: The Esplanade Terrace today; Top right: The Strand Hotel which was once called 'Elsinore'; Inset: Dr. William and Lady Wilde; Below right: The view of Bray Head from the Wilde's home at Esplanade Terrace c. 1900.

111

BRAY - DID YOU KNOW...?

County Wicklow · Ireland

braydidyouknow@gmail.com

"HEMPENSTALL...THE WALKING GALLOWS"

Lieutenant Edward Hempenstall was born in Newcastle, County Wicklow in the 1760s, By the 1790s Hempenstall's family were based in Sandymount Green, where they ran a school.

At a time when the average man was around five feet tall, Hempenstall was an amazing seven-foot giant, with strength to match. He was a notorious Lieutenant of the Loyalist Militias, charged with suppressing the increasingly active United Irishmen, in Wicklow.

If Hempenstall met a peasant who could not 'satisfactorily account for himself' he knocked him down with a blow of his fist, and then adjusting a noose around the prisoners neck, drew the rope over his own shoulders, and trotted about, the victim's legs dangling in the air, and his tongue protruding, until death at last put an end to the torture.

Above: Part of Hepenstal Terrace in Sandymount. Note the spelling.

In late May 1798, a witness saw a prisoner, worn out after a beating at the barrack yard, hoisted over Hempenstall's shoulders, choking and gulping until given a parting chuck; just to make sure his neck was broken.

There was a degree of justice in the end for Hempenstall. In 1800 he was afflicted with an infestation of lice, and his body was devoured from within. After twenty-one days of horrendous suffering, he died in excruciating agony.

Two lines of verse were composed on his death:

'Here lies the bones of Hempenstall,
Judge, jury, gallows, rope and all'.

Entertainers of Bygone Days (Part I of II)

Bray has always been well known for its public entertainers over the years, but some are lost to the shadows of distant memory. Here we have a small selection of the entertainers, musicians and the truly weird acts that have performed in Bray in days gone by...

Azigo Bay or **Ezigo Bey** was a performer of African origin who specialised in fire eating and fire walking on Bray Seafront near where Star Leisure now stands, in or around the 1940s. Licking red hot metal bars and walking on burning coals was his speciality. It is recorded that a local man watching the performance offered to try to 'lick the red hot iron' and ended up in the hospital with severe burns to his tongue for his trouble.

The Lilliputians were outside of the usual run of back-yard penny shows. The Lilliputians were a troupe of midgets who were billed as *'The Smallest People in the World.'* The 'Actors' were principally from Germany, Austria and Hungary, and they ranged in height from 28 to 38 inches. Their repertoire always included Gullivers Travels and they mostly performed outside Dawsons Amusements in a glass fronted box, not unlike a protected doll's house.

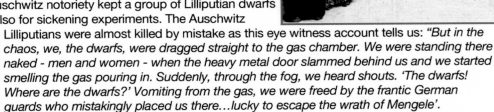

The infamous Dr. Josef Mengele of Auschwitz notoriety kept a group of Lilliputian dwarfs at the camp firstly for entertainment but also for sickening experiments. The Auschwitz

Lilliputians were almost killed by mistake as this eye witness account tells us: *"But in the chaos, we, the dwarfs, were dragged straight to the gas chamber. We were standing there naked - men and women - when the heavy metal door slammed behind us and we started smelling the gas pouring in. Suddenly, through the fog, we heard shouts. 'The dwarfs! Where are the dwarfs?' Vomiting from the gas, we were freed by the frantic German guards who mistakingly placed us there...lucky to escape the wrath of Mengele'.*

Just before the outbreak of World War II, the Lilliputian group who toured Bray left and returned to mainland Europe. So could it be possible that it was the same group of people who had the terrorising experience at the infamous Auschwitz Nazi camp were the same group that entertained the crowds on Bray's seafront? Perhaps we will never know...

to be continued...

Entertainers of Bygone Days (Part II of II)

Edgar Wilson Benyon or *'Same Man, Different Clothes'* (March 29, 1902 - Sept 14, 1978) was born in New Zealand and became one of New Zealand's greatest entertainers. He toured the world with his "One-man revue" featuring magic, ventriloquism, juggling, rag pictures, quick-change, contortions and impressions. Edgar would go through his illusions, changing his costume every ten minutes with the lead-in "same man different clothes" shouted out by the audience. He disclosed that he had about "25 tons of paraphernalia, enough to fill six railroad vans each 40 feet long".

When war broke out in 1939 and theatres were closed, the family moved to Ireland. Here the full evening show of magic was named 'Bam-Boo-Zalem' with Edgar's one-man variety act as its cornerstone. By now his daughter Doris was taking part in the show under the stage name Evelyn Talma. In 1943 she married an Irish army officer, Sean O'Hagan, who also became an integral part of the show. Edgar died in Queensland, Australia on 14 September 1978.

The Blind Fiddler of 'Fiddlers Bridge' Padraig O' Gradaigh was part of Bray's summer scene for over 40 years. It is thought that Padraig lost his sight through measles at the age of 13, and was advised by his local Parish Priest to take up the fiddle as an extra means of income.

Padraig travelled every summer from the Beara Peninsula in Cork to Bray and played his music to locals and visitors alike on the small bridge that overlooks the railway track as you make your way up Bray Head the bridge is known locally as *Fiddlers Bridge*.

On the 13th October 1941, Padraig died at number 25 Castle Street, Bray. His family took his remains home for burial at Ardrigole Church, Beara, Co. Cork.

Above: Bray Seafront at the height of the season, summer 1952 and a beach packed full of tourists, visitors and locals alike. The boats on the beach were for hire for a small fee you could be brought around Bray Head.

Right: A great photo from 1958 taken from Bray Head. Note all the green fields and open spaces around the town at the time.

BRAY *in the* **50s!**

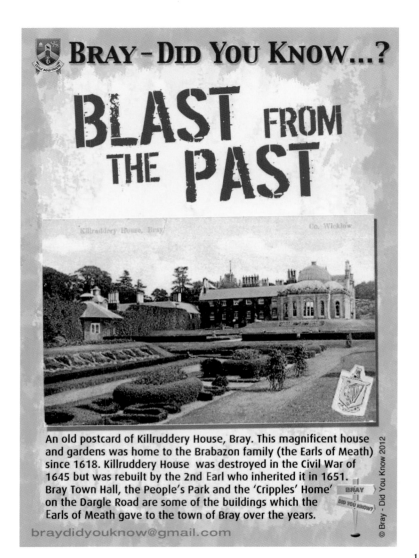

BLAST FROM THE PAST

Killruddery House, Bray.   Co. Wicklow

An old postcard of Killruddery House, Bray. This magnificent house and gardens was home to the Brabazon family (the Earls of Meath) since 1618. Killruddery House was destroyed in the Civil War of 1645 but was rebuilt by the 2nd Earl who inherited it in 1651. Bray Town Hall, the People's Park and the 'Cripples' Home' on the Dargle Road are some of the buildings which the Earls of Meath gave to the town of Bray over the years.

BRAY
DID YOU KNOW?

braydidyouknow@gmail.com

© Bray - Did You Know 2012

Killruddery House

An aerial photo of Killruddery House and Gardens.

BRAY - DID YOU KNOW...?

County Wicklow · Ireland

braydidyouknow@gmail.com

W.J. Owens of Bray   Part I of III

W.J.Owens opened for business in 1941 right in the middle of World War II, having had a shop in Albert Avenue for a number of years.

Due to the War stocks were very limited and it was not until the early 1950s that local business really picked up, due to the large influx of tourists from the UK in summertime, who purchased souvenirs jewellery and fishing tackle.

Once again, the avalability of toys, including the popular large metal Tri-Ang range, detailed toys from Dinky, Corgi and Matchbox, with model kits by Airfix and Revell and also Hornby train sets, Lego and Cindy dolls soon followed.

BRAY - DID YOU KNOW...?

County Wicklow · Ireland

braydidyouknow@gmail.com

W.J. Owens of Bray

Part II of III

The next big step in the business was to introduce photographic equipment, not only the leading camera brands such as Ashai Pentax, Minolta, Nikon, Olympus, Voiglander, Eumig and Fuji, but also the processing and darkroom equipment and chemicals for home processing. A film processing service was always readily available.

In the late 1960s the range of model aircraft was vastly expanded, and in 1974 Sean O'Hehir joined William Owens Senior and William Jnr in the business (pictured opposite) helping the tradition of providing the highest possible level of service to all their customers for the following 30 years.

W.J. Owens of Bray

Part III of III

Photographic supplies and Aero modelling formed the main business from 1980 with the range and selection of model kits, materials, paints, balsa, and a huge array of accessories, plus remote control equipment long regarded by modelers as the most extensive selection available in the country at the time.

This massive selection of parts and accessories, backed by well maintained stock levels, brought customers to Bray from all over Ireland. A fast mail order service was also available to both local and overseas customers alike.

Sadly, the decision to retire was taken in early 2004, and the business closed after 63 years of successful trading in June of that year.

BRAY – DID YOU KNOW...?

County Wicklow · Ireland

braydidyouknow@gmail.com

Duelling in Bray

In 1787 Sir John Conway Colthurst died at Old Connaught from wounds received in a duel a few days previously, when he had been hit during the third discharge of pistols.

In 1789 a duel was to be fought on Bray Beach – a popular area for duelling among the dunes and grass banks. After being assaulted in Dublin in 1791, John Philpot Curran, the eminent lawyer, challenged his assailant to a duel in Bray on the seafront. The aggressor, Mr Bingham, travelled to Bray where he made an abject apology, and both men returned to Dublin unharmed.

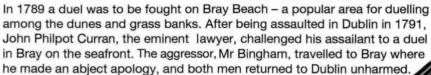

In 1797 the most sensational shots occurred between the young Earl of Meath and Captain Gore, at Cookstown Hill near Enniskerry. Lord Meath collapsed after being hit in the thigh and was brought to Powerscourt House. The surgeons were unable to extract the ball, removing only apart of his pantaloons from the wound. Lord Meath died some weeks later from septicaemia.

BRAY – DID YOU KNOW...?

County Wicklow · Ireland

braydidyouknow@gmail.com

St. Peter's Church in Little Bray *(Part I of III)*

Hidden away off the Dublin Road in Bray is the quaint little St. Peter's Church. Even though it was built in 1837, it didn't become a parish until Fr. James Healy was appointed in 1869. But its history goes back further because of the strange circumstances that led to its foundation. The story starts during the penal times in Dublin, around the year 1750 when a group of worshippers were attending Mass in a makeshift chapel on Townsend Street.

There was a violent storm which caused an overhead chimney stack to fall through the flimsy roof and a number of the congregation were killed and many injured. The major tragedy was reported in the popular press, but as the *Royal Dublin Society* were moving to new premises and were then situated close to Townsend Street, they donated part of their old site for the building of a small chapel in Westland Row, which was to be known as 'The Gentleman's Chapel'. The famous Daniel O'Connell heard Mass there when he was in Dublin and later on he purchased a new site for a large substantial building in Westland Row, later to be called St. Andrew's, and the Gentleman's Chapel was closed. There was a beautiful reredos in the old chapel and it was carefully stored away.

On the south side of Old Connaught Avenue in Little Bray, are the ruins of an old church surrounded by a cemetery - which has been used up to modern times. This is where Mass was celebrated in the past but like the rest of the buildings it decayed and was in ruins around about 1630 having suffered the same fate as all the others. Nearly two centuries later in 1810, it was decided to build another, this time at Crinken, on the site where the entrance to Shanganagh cemetery is now - a convenient location on the main Dublin Road between Shankill and Bray.

Opposite the church at Crinken there was a public house, there appears to have been a lot of trouble here, mostly on Sundays after Mass, and faction fighting became quite common with crowds from Bray and Shankill going out to Crinken and thrashing one another. Eventually the landlord could no longer bear with the carry on so he requested the priest, Father Sullivan, to leave. He was quite polite and reasonable as it appears that he allowed them four years to find another site, which they did in Little Bray on land belonging to a Mr. James Coghlan at Gurchen's Lane. The only sign of anything belonging to the little church at Crinken now is a large granite cross, quarried and carved in Glencree with the date 1810 at its base, which now stands in the old cemetery of St. Peter's near the gate at the Parish Hall.

to be continued...

Clockwise from top: Workmen standing at the entrance of St. Peter's Church back in 1837; The granite cross which belonged to the church at Crinken; The entrance to Shanganagh cemetery at the site of the Crinken church; A photo of St. Peter's Church before the major alterations in 2009.

BRAY – DID YOU KNOW...?

braydidyouknow@gmail.com

St. Peter's Church in Little Bray *(Part II of III)*

The reredos from the old 'Gentleman's Chapel' in Dublin were taken out of storage and placed in the church when it was completed and opened in 1837. The style of the interior was described as neo-classical and an imitation of the architecture of the ruins of the destroyed city of Pompeii - which had just then been discovered and had become all the new fashion for churches. The floorboards in the sanctuary were lifted a few years ago and underneath were found two panels, belonging to the original reredos, decorated with floral and Eucharistic symbols.

The Stations of the Cross are by the famous Irish painter George Collie R.H.A and are most extraordinary as, unlike most others, they are bright and colourful. Inside the porch is a holy water font presented by Father James Healy's sister in memory of him. The magnificent painting above the tabernacle, the crucifixion, is thought to be of Spanish origin and many centuries old.

This was one of the first churches to be built in south Dublin and north Wicklow after Catholic Emancipation. Like all the others it was removed from the main road and the 'Coach & Horses' public house was in front of it as 'The Coach Inn' pub is today.

The cemetery at the rear of the church was opened in 1842 and in 1905 it was reported to be full. Some of the walks were even used for graves. Adjoining land to the west of the Church was purchased for a new cemetery in 1905 and was consecrated by Most Rev. William Walsh, Archbishop of Dublin. The first person to be buried here is situated inside the main gates, the grave of a man who tragically lost his life in the explosion at the electric works (where *The Maltings* is situated now) in Bray on 10th July 1912. Land for an extension of the cemetery was obtained in 1952 by arrangement with the Council and part of the extension land had been ceded in exchange for a school site in the Palermo area. In the first six months of 1954 the new cemetery was enclosed and laid out at a total cost of £1,524, in 1959 the space around the Church and the cemetery paths were resurfaced. Many of the priests from the area or of the parish are buried here, including Canon Piggot who has inscribed on his tombstone "see you later".

to be continued...

Clockwise from left: A photo of the church interior c. 1940; A mass during the 100th Anniversary of St. Peter's; The holy water font in the porch of the church; The first grave of the new graveyard was in 1912; The east gable of the church before the renovations.

BRAY – DID YOU KNOW...?

County Wicklow · Ireland

braydidyouknow@gmail.com

St. Peter's Church in Little Bray *(Part III of III)*

Major renovations of St. Peter's Church took place in 2010/2011 the long awaited €2.7m changes included an entire new roof, gallery and double stairwells, a new sacristy, seating, heating system and new marble baptismal font and pulpit. Ceilings and walls were re-plastered, paintings were professionally restored, and new inside and outside lighting and C.C.T.V. was installed.

The Parish Hall also got a welcomed face-lift, with a new roof, furniture and equipment and a new two-storey modern extension to the north end. The churchyard got a new sewage system, and the old tarmac was substituted for new cobble-stones, safety rails, new trees and lighting. But due to the fact that the Church and the Parish Hall are both listed/protected buildings, the work had to be completed sensitively.

A dedication ceremony took place at the Church on Sunday 20 November 2011. Archbishop Diarmuid Martin celebrated Mass and blessed the new Parish Centre. St. Peter's Church in Little Bray, although still retaining its character and feel from bygone days, is now one of the most modern equipped churches in Ireland...a far cry from the church of 1863.

1: The new gallery under construction.
2: The altar end of the church.
3: Looking down the new church from the altar.
4: Photo taken from the back of church.
5: The new church today.

BRAY – DID YOU KNOW...?

County Wicklow · Ireland

braydidyouknow@gmail.com

Bray's Ancient Forest

Bray was once the site of a large forest which stretched out into what is now the Irish Sea until it was drowned by rising seas after the last Ice Age 7,000 years ago. As the climate changed and the sea levels began to rise, the coastline moved inland and the forest was lost under the sea.

The construction of Bray harbour between 1891 and 1897 changed the way the sand and sediment moved causing a drop in the level of the north beach, resulting in traces of the ancient forest emerging from the sand.

According to a project by students of Aravon School in the early 1980s, their research showed that an area extending from Bray's Northern Beach out into the sea was once the site of a Scotch pine forest, a species of tree not now native to this country. Careful collection of examination of samples from the beach, plus correspondence with the Royal College of Trees at Holloway in England, confirmed that the forest consisted of Scotch pine.

With the help of a present day undersea map of the sea off Bray Head, the students were able to trace the course of a valley which long ago contained much of the forest, left there after the flooding from the last ice age in about 5,000 B.C.

Some remains of the trees, including stumps and partly buried trunks, can still be found a few hundred yards from the north pier on the 'Back Strand' at very low tides today.

Top right: The petrified Scotch pine forest with an unfinished North Pier in the background;
Right: Three recent photos of partly sunken wood from the pine forest on the Back Beach.

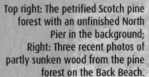

POSTCARDS FROM BRAY

A postcard (c. 1928) of the south end of the town looking north down Main Street.
Note how little traffic there was on the streets and how many people used bicycles.

BRAY - DID YOU KNOW...?

County Wicklow · Ireland

braydidyouknow@gmail.com

POSTCARDS FROM BRAY

Winter Sunrise, Bray Head, Co. Wicklow, Ireland.

Photo: D. Noble, John Hinde Studios.

A famous John Hinde postcard of Bray and Bray Head after a night of snow.
This photo was taken from the Ballyman Road near Old Connaught.

KINVARRA HOTEL,
DIRECTLY ON SEA FRONT.

Electric Lighting.   Moderate Charges.

Tariff on application—

Proprietress, Mrs. McHUGO.

LANCASHIRE & YORKSHIRE RAILWAY
Via Liverpool & Northwall; Via Holyhead & Northwall

BEAUTIFUL BRAY
QUEEN OF IRISH WATERING PLACES
GEM OF COUNTY WICKLOW
THE LOVELY GARDEN OF IRELAND

BRAY

CLIMATE PERFECT · SCENERY UNEQUALLED
GRAND MARINE PROMENADE A MILE LONG
FREE BATHING·GOLF·CRICKET·GAMES·FISHING
YACHTING·BOATING·MILITARY BANDS·CONCERTS
FREE GUIDE &c. FROM TOWN CLERK

A fine photo (right) c. 1910 and a photo (above) taken from the same place over one hundred years later – both taken from the balcony of the old Kinvarra Hotel, which is part of the Esplanade Terrace on the Strand Road. The terrace of four Victorian designed three-story houses were built in 1863 by Sir William Wilde (father of Oscar Wilde). The house is now called 'Kinvara House' and is a retirement home. In the background is the Esplanade Hotel with its prominent spires and the Strand Hotel which was also built by William Wilde in the 1850s.

The Gilt Spears

Prominent among the elevated objects seen from Bray are two mountains composed of quartz known as Little Sugarloaf and Big Sugarloaf. The two mountains were originally called the 'Gilt Spears' by the native Irish because the quartz rocks in the hills retained the light of the sun after the rest of the surrounding landscape was in darkness, and the mountains looked to them like gilted spears in the distance against the darkening skies.

   The name, 'Gilt Spears', which no other could be imagined more picturesque or significant, was altered by the English for the vulgar appellation of 'The Sugar loaves.'

   Perhaps they should be re-named to their original someday.

Little Sugarloaf Mountain

Big Sugarloaf Mountain

© Bray – Did You Know 2012

128

The Rathdown Union Workhouse *(Part 1 of 5)*

Designed by the Poor Law Commissioners' architect George Wilkinson, the Loughlinstown Workhouse was based on one of his standard designs.

Just over a couple of miles north of the town of Bray on the M11 is St. Columcille's Hospital in Loughlinstown. The hospital has treated thousands of people from all over the counties of Wicklow and Dublin for many decades now. Today it is hard to believe that in the mid-19th century it was one of the most hated places in the County, it was the Rathdown Union Workhouse, or popularly known as Loughlinstown Workhouse.

The Workhouse was built to a standard design in 1840 and cost £6,500 plus £1,100 fittings and fixtures. It was one of 130 workhouses built between 1839 and 1842. The Loughlinstown workhouse was built on an eight-acre site on land rented from Robert Tilly (at £7 an acre) west of the main Dublin to Wicklow Road. In 1838 an act for the relief of the destitute in Ireland, based on the New English Poor Law, was enacted. The scheme would augment private charities, which had made little impact on the appalling social conditions.

Three classes of poor were identified: the destitute unable to support themselves because of age, mental or physical handicap, or illness (these were eligible for a workhouse place); the poor but not destitute (these might receive assistance to emigrate); and poor, but not destitute and unsuitable for emigration (objects for charitable institutions).

The Board of Guardians, being landlords and local merchants, wished to save the ratepayers money by appointing a husband and wife theme as master and matron. Mr George and Kate Downes were elected master and matron in February 1841, but within a month representations were made about Mr Downes's unsuitable character. Mr Robert Leggett a retired constabulary sergeant from Dalkey became the first porter of the poorhouse at £15 per annum. George Mackay was elected clerk with a salary of £50 a year, later raised to £80.

Though originally approved for 800 inmates, the poorhouse was erected to accommodate 600 people. It first opened its doors on the 12th of October 1841   23 paupers were admitted, 16 Catholics and 7 Protestants. All were unable to support themselves. They were said to be suffering from Gravel and Piles, Paralytic sore legs and bad sight. After investigation by a parish warden the deserving poor presented themselves to the board of guardians, who made the final decision about admission. In an emergency the master admitted them, but only *"under circumstances so such extreme destitution as to induce him to fear that a refusal might be attended with fatal consequences"*.

to be continued...

The chapel is seperate at the north end.

The Rathdown Union Workhouse *(Part 2 of 5)*

Families were split up on admission, with women and girls housed in the left side of the building and men and boys in the right side. The exercise and the work yards were also segregated. When Mary Kelly presented herself at the door at midnight on 31 December 1842, recommended not only by the Superintendent of the Kingstown police but by two wardens, Downes turned her away because of the "unreasonableness of the hour". The Poor Law Commissioners reprimanded the master and wished to have him dismissed. The guardians, fearing disruption, pleaded successfully for clemency. The treatment of Downes stands in sharp contrast with the way paupers were sent away for breaking the workhouse rules.

All inmates were obliged to work for their keep. The women nursed the sick, cooked, cleaned, repaired workhouse uniforms, which resembled convicts' clothing and had to be returned when discharged. Men and boys who 'went over the wall' in

This 1907 OS map shows the workhouse (yellow), the chapel (green), the burial grounds (pink) and the fever hospital (orange); the Dublin – Wicklow Road is in blue.

workhouse jackets and trousers were frequently jailed for this offence. The men grew potatoes and cabbages, some of which were sold. They were also engaged in breaking stone for roads, making coconut matting, grinding wheat into flour, and picking oakum, which consisted of unravelling old rope, so the fibres could be used in caulking ships timbers. Men were not allowed to deposit their families in the workhouse and remain outside themselves. Equally, people were discharged only if they took all their dependents.

In the first years there were about 250 inmates in Loughlinstown (for the half-year ending in September 1843, 158 of the paupers came from Bray). After that the numbers rose steadily to 447 in March 1845.

The Rathdown guardians had adopted a proper diet, which was conducive to anaemia, lethargy and scurvy, all of which occurred in Loughlinstown. In practice, however, the menus were modified due to rising numbers and a shortage of union funds. Portions became smaller and Indian meal replaced the diseased potato. Porridge, bread and milk formed the staple workhouse diet, bread was often delivered too light, the milk unfit for human consumption. Only meat of the cheapest kind found its way into the soup, which also

A typical scene at the gates of a workhouse. contained a few vegetables, usually of poor quality.

to be continued...

BRAY - DID YOU KNOW...?

County Wicklow · Ireland

braydidyouknow@gmail.com

The Rathdown Union Workhouse *(Part 3 of 5)*

Fruit, vegetables, eggs and butter – not to mention luxuries like sugar and tea – were generally not consumed by paupers. The meat for soup (oxheads, trimmings) and the officers' rations were due to be delivered early on board meeting days, but frequently arrived late at night to disguise its inferior quality and make inspection impossible. The gastronomic highlights of the year were the Easter and Christmas dinners of bacon and cabbage, with beer from Bray Brewery. But the quality and quantity of food would slump even further as the years would pass.

The paupers dined off wooden tables and sat on forms. Their meals were taken in absolute silence, except when the master read the draconian workhouse rules to the mostly illiterate inmates. Besides corporal punishment for the boys, children and adults were frequently deprived of meals. The dormitories were later crammed with wooden bedsteads and sleeping platforms. The straw frequently crawled with ticks and fleas. Iron beds came later. Any contact between married couples was frustrated. Life inside the prison-like walls was so lacking in emotional and spiritual warmth that many preferred taking to the roads than accept pauper status.

Before the Famine, people entered Loughlinstown for the winter – the first family on the register was Judith Manley, her husband William, and their 8 children, from Bray – they left in spring. The workhouse was regarded as a last resort by the weakest members of society: unmarried mothers with "bastards", abandoned wives and children, orphans, the elderly, the chronically ill, the physically and mentally handicapped. No treatment was provided for the mentally ill, who were confined in "idiot cells" when Richmond Lunatic Asylum (now Grangegorman) in Dublin was overcrowded. At one stage 14 lunatics escaped from Loughlinstown and were at large for some weeks.

From late 1844 onwards isolated cases of fever occurred and, as the Famine crisis worsened, the administration of the workhouse began to slide towards chaos. By March 1844 there were 453 paupers in Loughlinstown. A year later 63 of the 447 inmates were in the poorhouse hospital. In December 1846 the guardians stated: "this workhouse is now full". Nevertheless, numbers rose to 700 by February 1847, which was known as 'Black 47'. From 1848 additional accommodation had to be provided as the numbers rose to 776, which was done by appropriating the workhouse stables; attics were eventually used as dormitories; some of the sleeping platforms can still be seen in the Hospital attics today. *to be continued...*

TOWNSHIP OF RATHDOWN
Extracts from the Order of the POOR LAW BOARD.

PUNISHMENTS

FOR

MISBEHAVIOUR OF THE PAUPERS

IN THE WORKHOUSE

Left: Birr workhouse dining hall; Top Left: The women wore prison-like uniforms at the workhouse; Above: A typical iron bed used in the mid 1800s.

BRAY - DID YOU KNOW...?

County Wicklow · Ireland

braydidyouknow@gmail.com

The Rathdown Union Workhouse *(Part 4 of 5)*

The construction of Loughlinstown workhouse quickly proved defective. The catalogue of complaints included: faulty chimneys, leaking roofs, faulty water and sewerage systems. This was not surprising as the guardians invariably selected the cheapest candidates for jobs. Throughout this period about double the number who gained admission had applied. Men slept in the stables and many of the destitute could be given only one night's accommodation. The pressure on space was such that the original building was enlarged to hold 680 people, while a new workhouse for 550 was completed. It was from only this period was it possible to relieve the poor in their own homes rather than have them enter the abhorred workhouse, starving and ill. Overcrowding and fear of an epidemic forced the authorities to modify their harsh economic doctrines and introduce outdoor relief. The deprivation endured by many people in the union increased the likelihood of famine fever (a general term covering typhus, relapse fever, scarlatina, smallpox, dropsy and dysentery).

A system to treat fever patients was put in place, which the guardians arranged with a colleague, Dr. Plant of the Rathdown Fever Hospital (better known as Bray Fever Hospital). Fever cases were transferred directly from their homes to Bray in a 'covered vehicle' built specially for this purpose. Paupers who developed a contagious disease while in Loughlinstown were also conveyed to the hospital. But soon after, this system broke down.

Temporary fever sheds were erected behind the poorhouse, and soon contained 50 patients. Rain leaked through within weeks of completion and on at least one occasion patients had to be evacuated. In February 1848 the number of fever cases had risen to 91, and as the fever raged, demoralisation and chaos reached a climax in the workhouse. Maria Walshe, the paid nurse in charge, was so drunk in February 1848 that she had to be dismissed. A pauper nurse, Mary Byrne, was discovered in the fever sheds engaged in "improper conduct" with Edward Reilly; both were discharged. Fever diseases gradually tapered off in the latter half of the year and only a handful of cased occurred in 1849.

Left and Below Right: Women and men of the workhouse in Cootehill, Co. Cavan. Below Left: The children's ward in Belfast Union Workhouse c.1895.

Small-scale pilfering had always taken place in the workhouse, but during the worst years of 1847-8 a breakdown in discipline occurred. A pauper was discovered cutting the union mark off linen, sacks of clothing (destined for the pawnbroker) were thrown over the wall, and some inmates scaled the boundary to bring tea and sugar into the poorhouse. Nurses and paupers vanished into the village with stolen goods (including the master and matron's clothing on one occasion). Eventually, a night watch of paupers was formed to guard the workhouse property.

to be continued...

The Rathdown Union Workhouse *(Part 5 of 5)*

Photo courtesy of Billy Byrne

A panoramic view of the burial ground behind St. Columcilles Hospital.

All pretence at work was given up, the house fell into a dirty, neglected state, and a picture emerges from the records of food, linen and clothing shortages, filthy bedstraw, overflowing sewers and foul hospital wards. At the same time LeBel's (the now master) clothing and provision accounts were fraudulent – an estimated 2,331 articles of clothing disappeared. He was eventually dismissed.

Efforts were made to restore order in 1849. A solitary confinement cell was situated in the new water tower and the paupers returned to work. Agricultural instruction was started for the boys. The guardians purchased an additional six acres and a permanent fever hospital was completed on this site in 1849. Of this building only the mortuary stands today. Initially, dead paupers were interred in their own graveyards, but in 1843 a 'burial ground for unclaimed paupers at the rear of the deadhouse' (area 8532 sq. ft.) was consecrated – nothing remains of this burial ground today. In 1845 about three inmates died each week; this figure rose to ten in 1847. Some were claimed by relatives and this avoided the stigma of a pauper's grave, but fever victims had to be buried in Loughlinstown. A new paupers' graveyard was opened in 1848, the original one being full. During the period covered in this article alone, between 1,500 and 2,500 people were buried in Loughlinstown.

One would never know that there is a burial ground at the rere of the hospital. It stood neglected and overgrown for many years, but members of the 51st Ballybrack Scout Troop managed to clean up the area in 1992. Several monuments stand here, including a large celtic cross which reads: *"Sacred to the memory of the Rev. Edward W. Burton, for 22 years Chaplin of the Rathdown Union Workhouse, who departed this life 3rd May, 1890 aged 77 years. Thanks be unto God for his unspeakable gift. 2 Cor. IX Chapter 15 Ver."* There is also a damaged headstone which reads: *"Erected by the Officers of the Rathdown Union, in greatful memory of Robert Sharpe, who died 5th October 1888, aged 48 years."* Another monument commemorates the 150th Anniversary of the Famine (see below).

"The short and simple annals of the poor" are recorded by the rows of almost forgotten paupers' graves behind St. Columcille's Hospital. They are part of our heritage, they lie forgotten. But deserve to be remembered.

Right: An old headstone with an inscription too hard to decipher;
Far right: This stone marks the 150th Anniversary of the Hospital. It reads:
'St. Columcilles Hospital 1841 – 1991 150th ANNIVERSARY
This stone was dedicated by Sister Angelis Matron of the hospital from 1974 - 1991
To the memory of all those interred here. The noble ones of other times sleep here,
quiet be thy voice they would not be disturbed. Pain and hunger gone, they feel not
winters cold. The shepherd has them now, safe within his fold. 12th October 1991.'

Thanks to Billy Byrne for his contribution to this feature.

Victorian Cutbacks: The Nightlodgers at the Workhouse *(Part I of II)*

In a rare travelogue published in Germany in 1837 Karl von Hailbronner describes his arrival in Kingstown (Dun Laoghaire) harbour:
" . . . the whole wall and stairs at the landing place were covered with half-naked people, insufficiently covered with rags, all of whom rushed towards us with wild screams, grabbed our possessions and ran off. Each had taken only one piece of luggage and by the time we had been able to step out of the ship everything had vanished. I confess such moments are not among the most pleasant of one's travels".

The German found his luggage arranged neatly beside the locomotive of the Kingstown to Dublin Railway. He marvelled at the honesty of the poor people. This impression was confirmed during his travels in County Wicklow. Hailbronner wrote on the eve of the Famine; his description gives an idea of how desperate the state of the country must have been ten years later.

Undoubtedly the most unfortunate category of poor were the 'travelling strangers': those who had been forced to leave their homes and take to the roads in search of employment, but more often reduced to begging. The vast crowds of wandering beggars during the Famine years faced death by slow starvation, exposed to the weather and likely to contract fever. The travelling poor were frequently admitted to workhouses as 'nightlodgers'. In Loughlinstown they were given a night's shelter in the stables, some straw to lie on and in harsh weather 'a little fire' was permitted by the Rathdown guardians. At one stage the nightlodgers received a workhouse supper and breakfast the next morning, but due to the hordes of destitute travellers and increasing administrative chaos the poor-law guardians tried to restrict expenditure.

The nightlodgers were soft targets for cutbacks. The proposals made in the document published here for the first time were implemented. On 1st December 1849 the workhouse Master refused to admit six applicants. The travelling paupers spend the harsh night outside the gates of Loughlinstown; by morning they were in such a condition that they had to be admitted to hospital. At this time the workhouse bread was particularly unwholesome, some inmates had contracted bowel complaints from it and others refused to eat it. In February 1850 the guardians decreed that the bread which the medical officer had condemned be 'given to night lodgers on condition that they should not return'.

While the population of Ireland declined by 20 per cent during the Great Famine, the Rathdown Union was one of the few places to record an increase. In 1841 it contained 44,505 people, but by 1851 this number had risen to 48,294. This can be explained by the migration eastward from the famine-stricken western seaboard. The report of the Poor Law Commissioners published in 1855 suggests that many of the homeless who survived had settled in the east.

The tone of this document is one of Victorian self-righteousness and hypocrisy. The guardians, eager to save their fellow ratepayers additional expenditure and in panic at the huge influx, did not distinguish between the dispossessed and a small element of tough vagrants.

to be continued...

Victorian Cutbacks: The Nightlodgers at the Workhouse *(Part II of II)*

Report of the Sub Committee appointed to consider the best mode of remedying the evils arising out of the admission of travelling paupers into the Workhouse for one night only.

Your Committee after giving their anxious consideration to the above subject find it extremely difficult to suggest an effectual remedy for the evils so justly complained of without recommending such a change in the present system as might subject the Board to the charge of harshness or inhumanity. They would however venture to advise the Guardians to close the gates every night at 9 o'clock and receive no paupers into the house after that hour except under great emergency and as it is not unreasonable to presume that poor persons moving for bonafide purposes from one part of the Country to another have means either by begging or otherwise of procuring at least a scanty subsistence they cannot help thinking that there would be no particular hardship confining them to one meal during their stay in the Workhouse. Which meal they think should be given in the morning before they leave the establishment while the one which they have latterly received at night may be withheld' And as the regular inmates of the workhouse have but 2 meals in 24 hours they cannot conceive why the migratory pauper (a very doubtful character) should have 2 meals within half that space of time.

The Board of Guardians of Dungarvan Workhouse pose for a photo.

Your Committee have consulted the Union Inspector on this subject and have to report that he approves of the above suggestion.

It should be recollected that all which originally sought for by this class of paupers and all that their case seemed to require was a mere nights lodging. and that for some time after orders were first given to allow them that accommodation they received nothing more. The evil however has now become one of such magnitude that your committee fear it cannot be effectually grappled with without still more stringent means and they think that every able body wandering pauper whether male or female admitted for one night only should if possible be obliged to perform a moderate quantity of work before receiving the morning meal, which work should not be required to perform if they choose to leave the house without that meal.

Your Committee are quite aware of the responsibility to which the Master may subject himself by refusing admission to weak or destitute persons who may apply at the workhouse for a nights lodging yet they are of opinion that the indiscriminate reception of all persons who choose to apply for it should not be allowed and that he ought to exercise much caution as to whom he admits and to reject all those who in his deliberate judgement are not really destitute or in need of the accommodation they seek.

Nor can your Committee think that the Master could be blamed for rejecting such applicants as may appear strong and healthy but be this as it may it is obvious that the present system should be changed not only because it is attended with much additional expense to the rate payers and greatly increases the labour of the officers of the establishment but because it encourages and tends to perpetuate those baneful habits of vagrancy and idleness to which too many of the Irish peasantry are addicted.

Signed this day 28th Nov. 1849
Thos. Dixon – Chairman

By Eva O' Cathaoir

BRAY • NOW AND THEN

County Wicklow • Ireland

The National Sealife Centre (aquarium) now stands on the site of the Ladies' Baths, or old Bray Baths, on the Esplanade. They were built in 1878 by the Bray Pavilion Company – its prospectus noting the 'deficiency in provision for amusement and recreation of visitors' to Bray.

Note the showman's booths on the Esplanade and the old lady, who sold fresh fruit, sitting beside the entrance to the baths. Of course there were no 'Pay & Display' meters either!

136

BRAY - DID YOU KNOW...?

County Wicklow · Ireland

braydidyouknow@gmail.com

The Albert Walk *(Part I of II)*

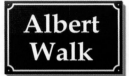

Albert Walk

The Albert Walk is a pedestrian walkway, which stretches from Albert Avenue to the railway station. Once called 'Albert Lane', it was renamed Albert Walk in 1886 and is on the Ordnance Survey maps of 1909 as Albert Walk.

Like most of the town, there was not much on Albert Walk before the railway came to Bray, but as it was, and still is, a quick route to the seafront from the station, it was always bound to become a top spot for traders aiming their trade at tourists and day trippers from Dublin on heading to and from Bray seafront.

GOOD NEWS!
MICK'S AMUSEMENTS
ALBERT WALK :: BRAY
BEST KNOWN :: BEST LIKED.
BE SURE AND VISIT
"SORRENTO CAFE"
AT THE CORNER.
OPEN FOR THE SEASON

Business on the Albert Walk did very well during the summer seasons, especially from the 1940s to the 1960s. In the early days *Wallace Brothers* had a demanding coal merchants business and also owned their own schooner at Bray's harbour. Miss O'Donohue had a drapers shop, while next door J. Plunkett had his plumbing and gas fitting business. There was *Henry's*; a jewellery and fancy goods shop, there was also *Donnelly's Tobacconist* and *Foster's* had a thriving hairstyling business for years.

At the top end of the Albert Walk was *Donnelly's Hairdressing Salon*, next door was the popular *Mannion's Café* and two doors from there was *Lyon's Café* - both were never short of customers.

Up to the 1950s and 1060s there was Mr & Mrs Harte's *Gift Shop* which sold jewellery and name brooches, which were 'made while-U-wait'. *The Sorrento Café* was the first premises you would meet on the corner at Albert Avenue end, which sold tea, coffee, cakes and sandwiches etc. Then there was *Mick's Amusements* whose Pongo games attracted many a passer by...

Our Egregious Guide Books

BRAY, Co. Wicklow

Albert Walk, Bray. 'Gate way to the Brighton of Ireland. Bray abounds in numerous delightful walks where the visitor can enjoy the charming mountain scenery of Wicklow and the Golden Vale...'

RICE High-Class Confectioner, Tobacconist, Stationer, Newsagent.
TOYS :: :: :: FANCY GOODS
9 Albert Walk - BRAY

to be continued...

Left: A drawing of the Albert Walk from a guide book;
Top right: A photo of the Albert Walk c. 1958; Centre right: An early photo of the top end of the Albert Walk.

BRAY - DID YOU KNOW...?

County Wicklow · Ireland

The Albert Walk (Part II of II)

The Cooke family ran the well known *Manhattan Grill and Soda Fountain* on the walk which always did a roaring trade as did *Manhattan Amusements*. At no. 9 *Rice's* shop sold confectionery, tobacco, stationery and fancy goods while upstairs there was a ladies hairdressing parlour that was never short of business.

"Best Pong Games In Bray" is what the *Monaco Amusement Centre* advertised and the neon sign of *Eddie's Amusements* was visible from the top end of the street. *Silvercraft Ltd* of 10B Albert Walk made and sold solid silver trinkets from their premises and by mail order while photographer Hedley Wright developed film for tourists from no. 2 Peader Byrne and Harry Dawson who took photographs of tourists for a small fee were two of his best customers.

P.J. Cullen Victualler sold prime lamb and beef and Candeli's Restaurant cooked it well with chips and peas! The wonderful smell of fish n' chips came from next door's outlet and the queues sometimes reached as far as the *Rock Shop*, who sold all flavours and sizes of Bray rock. Near to them was *Batesman's* tobacco and confectionery shop, who like Mr. Wright had a very good film and processing business. But, if that was not enough, *Henry & Rose* hand opened a fantastic fish n' chip shop round the corner at the top of the walk and down at the other end the *Roxy Cinema* - later to become the *Panorama Theatre* – featured all the best films and had an entrance on the walk, their main door being around the corner on Albert Avenue.

However as soon as the era of the traditional seaside holiday ended in the late 1960s and early 1970s, the Albert Walk was about to change forever. The cafés and wonderful little shops that sold the ice cream, souvenirs, fish n' chips, etc closed one by one. The pedestrianised walkway at the centre of Bray's nascent Chinatown has still got some good shops including restaurants, Asian food supplies, casinos and a coffee shop – but the bustling tourists and character of the old Albert Walk is probably gone forever.

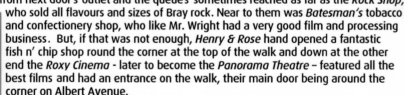

Monaco Amusement Centre

for BEST PONGO GAMES IN BRAY

Ireland's Most Luxurious Arena

CASH PRIZES GUARANTEED SECOND TO NONE

Under Personal Supervision

Clockwise from left: P.J. Cullen's Victualler shop; Customers order their Christmas turkey and meat at Cullen's; A large sample of Bray Rock at the 'Rock Shop'; A family photo outside the 'Manhattan Amusements'; 'Candeli's' ready to open for business.

BRAY - DID YOU KNOW...?

BLAST FROM THE PAST

An advertising poster which was used in Britain to advertise Bray as the 'Queen of Irish Watering Places'.

Back in the early days of our Grand Marine Promenade, Bray was one of the top resorts to visit in the whole of the British Isles in fact, it is why the resort got the name of 'The Brighton of Ireland'.

Every hotel and guesthouse on the seafront and in the town were always full and one would have even had a hard time trying to book a room in advance.

Yes, Bray was once famous for its resort, mountain scenery, fresh sea and country air, its location and of course, its mile-long promenade. Back then, Bray had it all.

braydidyouknow@gmail.com

© Bray - Did You Know 2012

139

The Brighton of Ireland

An early postcard of the promenade and esplanade c. 1900.

BRAY - DID YOU KNOW...?

County Wicklow · Ireland

braydidyouknow@gmail.com

POSTCARDS FROM BRAY

Construction on a tower at the Church of the Most Holy Redeemer was completed in October 1952 at a cost of £3,300. The cost of rehanging the bell was £400. In 1958 it was decided to begin rebuilding the old portion of the church.

The roof had deteriorated to such an extent that it had to be replaced. Plans were drawn up and a roof to correspond with the newer roof was replaced by Messrs. Du Moulin contractors at a total cost of £8,126.11.3d. Rebuilding of the walls was completed in 1959 at a total cost of £4,006.

In the summer of 1961 it was decided to rebuild the front of the church and the tower to harmonise with the Romanesque style of Dr. Donnelly's church. The Tower was put to contract and the tender of Mr. P. Mullen at £19,000 accepted. This work on the tower and new front was completed in 1965.

The huge granite pillars and entrance gates, along with the existing three flights of steps were removed, being replaced by two flights of steps, thus giving much easier access to the new porticos of the Church, with its magnificent arched entrance, ceremonial door and St. Catherine's window.

Church of the Redeemer, Bray, Co. Wicklow

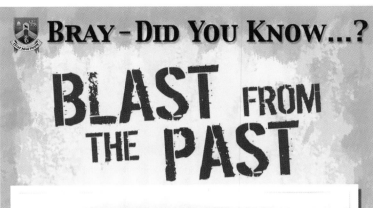

BLAST FROM THE PAST

A photo c. 1930 of Wallace's coal yard at the railway end of the north pier at Bray Harbour. Coal was brought in by coalboats, mostly from Wales and Scotland by Wallace Brothers Ltd. and delivered all around the town by horse and dray, and later by truck. Wallace Bros. also had an office located at No. 2 Albert Walk for many years.

braydidyouknow@gmail.com

BRAY
DID YOU KNOW?

© Bray - Did You Know 2012

Wallace Bros. at the Harbour

A Wallace Company collier unloading on the north pier c. 1913.

POSTCARDS FROM BRAY

Main Street, Bray, Co. Wicklow

A postcard of Bray Main Street c. 1950. Bray was well known for its great shops and stores. There were Alex Findlaters Butchers, Wilde's Tobacconist, Murdoch's Hardware, Egg Chicks, Kavanagh's, Lochners Butchers, Raverty's Medical Hall and many more.

BRAY – DID YOU KNOW...?

County Wicklow · Ireland

braydidyouknow@gmail.com

SHIPWRECKS OFF BRAY

Before the harbour was built at the mouth of the Dargle River in 1897, there was many a tragedy in which a lot of local and foreign seamen lost their lives to the many voracious storms that, even today, hit our eastern seaboard. Many of the vessels were driven ashore and smashed against the rocks, some were just seeking refuge during a storm. Many survived, but sadly, many of them did not. The following is a list of shipwrecks that were recorded off our town of Bray...

17th January, 1744 'Francis': From Bordeaux was lost as well as another French sloop (small ship with one mast): several were lost from the sloop.

20th October, 1781 Two Ships: Two coasters (coastal traders) sank off Bray Head. (ships which traded along the coast)

3rd February, 1784 'Friendship': Driven ashore off Bray, the cargo of oil and port wine from Oporto in Portugal - to the value of £4,000 - were carried off by locals.

28th November, 1790: Four Coasters: They were caught on the Lee shore between Dalkey and Bray. Two men and a boy were lost.

25th March, 1810 'Invincible': Was lost off Bray Beach. She was from Aberystwyth from Liverpool, England.

25th April, 1819 'Friends Of Liverpool': Lost in sight of Bray. The Captain, his two and a half year old son and a seaman were lost. The mate and the Captain's wife survived.

24th November, 1824 'Francis': Wrecked and went to pieces but the crew were saved. She carried beans and wheat from Bray to Liverpool.

11th October, 1836 'Erne Of Wicklow': Beached at Quin's Ground Bray. Saved by Coastguard.

16th March, 1844 Coal Sloop: Wrecked off Bray.

4th November, 1844 'Sovereign': No details available, but was wrecked off Bray.

12th November, 1852 'Lady Harriet': Wrecked off Bray.

27th November, 1858 River Steamer: Wrecked off Bray Head and went to bits off Greystones. The Coastguard were unable to name her.

31st October, 1863 Schooner: At the height of a storm a schooner was wrecked on Bray Beach. The crew was rescued.

26th October, 1864: - Unknown: Wreckage came ashore covered with barnacles between Bray & Wicklow harbour.

27th January, 1873 - 'Pimorrero': The Italian Barque (sailing ship) stranded on the Dublin side of Bray Head. The Coastguard fired their life-saving rockets to the wreck with instructions in French and English, which were not understood. The crew were rescued and taken by a tug to Kingstown (Dun Laoghaire). The 800 ton vessel carried a cargo of grain.

1st September, 1875 - 'Vanguard': The iron-hulled British battleship was sunk after a collision with 'The Iron Duke' off the Kish lightship. No loss of life.

30th September, 1876 - 'Leonie': The Leonie struck the shore off the former site of Martello Tower No.3 (north of Bray Harbour). She capsized at the mouth of the Bray River.

The H.M.S. Vanguard

20th March, 1906 - 'Velenheli': A coal vessel ran aground near Bray harbour.

31st January, 1926 - 'Marie Celine': A ketch (two-masted sailing boat) that was wrecked near Bray harbour.

17th October, 1936 'Erne': A sloop, which ran aground at Bray.

4th March, 1947 'M.V. Bolivar': On her maiden voyage to South America from Norway, she struck The Kish bank and was stranded. All the crew and passengers were saved. Wreckage and cargo (mainly leather) was washed ashore at Killiney, Bray and Greystones.

BRAY – DID YOU KNOW...?

County Wicklow · Ireland

braydidyouknow@gmail.com

The fate of the five Bray fishermen

On 28 February 1811 a boat's crew, consisting of six men from Bray, left the beach at Bray and set out on a fishing trip to sea; on the following morning the boat was perceived at anchor, two miles off the land. When conceiving them to be in distress, a boat – double manned – went to their assistance but to their inexpressible sorrow they found only one of the fishermen alive, the other five having perished, in consequence of the extreme hardships and fatigue they had undergone the preceding night during a raging storm.

Their names are: Richard Gary (47), leaving a widow and four children, the eldest of whom is not 10 years old; William Redmond (45), leaving a widow and two children; Denis Doyle (28) leaving a widow and two children, his widow far advanced in pregnancy; Henry Kirley (32), the only support of a widowed mother and two sisters; Thomas Seymour (17), the principal support of his parents and five young children.

Upon the industry of these men their families almost exclusively depended for the necessities of life, and it is hoped, that an appeal to the wealthy, in whose service such valuable lives may justly be said to have been lost, will not be ineffectual.

Donations will be thankfully received by Rev. J.W. Orsby, Glebehouse, Bray; and Mr. John Quin, Bray.

Article taken from a national newspaper a few days after the tragedy.

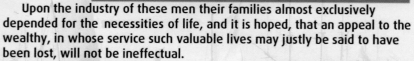

Left: Fishermen at their boats along Bray's seafront c. 1890.
Top: Before the harbour was built, Bray fishermen kept their boats along the beach on the seafront.

The Town Hall, Main Street, Bray   Co. Wicklow

A postcard (right) from c. 1895 shows the top end, or south end of the town. Note the wall of the Parochial House where the Rev. Donnelly PP resided, now the Civic Centre. Next door at no. 45 was George Pierce's grocer and vintner and was for many years in the town. King's Butchers were here for a few years after, eventually the premises becoming a branch of the *Bank of Ireland* (top) and was recently demolished and the new existing building was built. Above *The Ardmore Bar* (next door at no. 46) recently re-opened again after having being closed for a period.

Enniskerry

Enniskerry village centre today and yesterday. The Clock Tower, built at the expense of the 6th Viscount Powerscourt, was presented to the Village on St. Patrick's Day in 1843. A very interesting feature of the monument is that its base is made in the shape of a shamrock.

The school behind the tower was built in 1818 and the nearby house, 'Ferndale', built c.1850, served as the schoolmaster's house. One hundred years ago the village was as self-sufficient as Bray was at the time; it had everything that was required to exist on its own with a population of over two hundred.

The Quinsborough Road War Memorial - *Part I of II*

The War memorial cross on the Quinsborough Road at the Carlisle Grounds is situated on a site donated by the Dublin and South Eastern Railway Company. The cross stands on three tiers of steps, with some 150 names inscribed on bronze tablets, set into six panels. It was erected in 1920 on a grassy plot, which faced the Princess Patricia Hospital (International Hotel) – now the site of a leisure centre.

Viscount Powerscourt, the chairman of the local War committee, favoured a cross 22 feet high, but when this proved too expensive the committee settled on 17 feet 6 inches. It cost £550 and was executed by C.W. Harrison and Sons of Great Brunswick Street, Dublin. The architect Sir Thomas Deane designed many of these pseudo-Celtic crosses, as well as a number of War memorial buildings including the Trinity College of Honour.

The inscription of the front panel reads:

"This cross is erected by the people of Bray in loving and grateful memory of the brave soldiers, sailors and airmen who have given their lives for their country in the great war".

No separate memorial to the dead of the Second World War was erected in Bray. An inscription at the foot of the pedestal simply adds:

"Also in memory of those who gave their lives in the cause of freedom 1939 – 1945".

to be continued...

The Quinsborough Road War Memorial - *Part II of II: Remembrance Day Parade*

On November 17th 1924, huge crowds lined the Quinnsborough Road for the Remembrance Celebrations and wreath laying at the War Memorial. A marching band led the War Veterans, many displaying their medals. A Boy Scout stands with a flag and bowed head in respect while a section of the crowd of Veterans observe a moment's silence as the Last Post is played. Wreaths are placed at the base of the War Memorial.

BRAY – DID YOU KNOW...?

County Wicklow · Ireland

braydidyouknow@gmail.com

*This cross is erected by the people of Bray in loving and grateful memory of the brave sailors, soldiers
and airmen who gave their lives for their country in the Great War.
Also in the memory of those who gave their lives in the cause of freedom 1939-1945.*

Rev. Armar Acton
Pte. Richard Barrington
Pte. Thomas E. Boyd
Captain Hon. Ernest Brabazon D.S.O
James Breen
L/Cpl Patrick Breen
Pte. William Brennock
Pte. John Charles Brewster
Pte. Joseph Brien
Pte. Michael Brien
Pte. Michael Kinsella
Sgt. John Kitson
Pte. Frank Knox
Pte. Albert E. Langidge
Rifleman John langton
Pte. Patrick Joseph Langton
Pte. Henry Lawrence
Riffleman John Ledwidge
Lieut. Joseph Bagnall l.ee
Capt. Robert Ernest Lee
Sgt. George Lucas M.M.
Rifleman John Madden
Capt. & Q/Mas. T B Mahoney M.C.
Henry John Malley

Pte. John Manley
Captain John F. Marfyr
Pte. Henry Mason
Lieut. Douglas Slade Maunsell
Pte. John Messitt
Cpl Arthur Meyer
R.S.M. Ernest Mever
Patrick Mooney
Capt. M. Alwynne Moses
Pte. Edward Dalton
Comdr. Arthur T. Darley R.N.
Lieut. Col. John E.C. Darley
Pte. John F. Darlington
Pte. David Davies
Pte. Thomas Dawson
Lieut. Thomas Alex David Deane
Lieut. Fergus Dobbin
Lieut. Robert A. S. Dobbin
Pte. Henry Donegan
Cpl. Thomas L. Doolan
Cpl. William Doolan
Sgt. John McKenna
L/Cpl Bartholomew Naylor
Signaller Thomas Neill

Pte. Robert Howlett Nicholson
Pte. James Nolan
Pte. Michael Nordell
Capt. Frederick A. O'Donnell
Joseph O'Connor
Rifleman George O'Reilly
Pte. James O'Reilly (Reilly)
Petty Officer Thomas Pattison
Pte. Joseph J Raverty
Pte. John Redmond
Patrick Reilly
Lieut. Robert A. Revell
Edward Rice
Lieut. J. Vanston Richards
L/Cpl H. N. W. Roberts
Lieut. John Rogers
C.S.M. Francis J. M. Sherry D.C.M.
Rifleman John Sinnott
Rifleman Thomas Sinnott (John)
2nd Lieat. William Godfrey Skelton
Capt. Algemon Smyth
Pte. Digby M. Starkey
Pte. William Stedman
Cpl. J. N. Foster Strickland

Lieut. George Taylor
L/Cpl William Thompson
Pte. John Tiernan
R.S.M. James Toole
L/Cpl Michael J. Toole
Pte. Patrick Toole
Pte. William Toole
Pte. Thomas Traynor
Capt. J. A. St Leger Tredennick
A/BRD John Turner
Pte. Joseph Vance
Cpl. William Vance
Capt. Richard H. Waller
Pte. Alexander Watt
John Reginald Whitsitt
Capt. Armar Lowry C. Wintle M.C.
Col. Fitzhardinge Wintle
Edward N. Heatley

*Let us not
forget them*

149

MADE IN BRAY

ARDMORE STUDIOS IRELAND

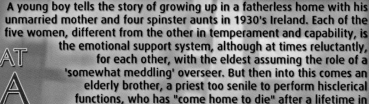

"A triumph"

The love that they shared, and the summer that changed them forever.

DANCING AT LUGHNASA
A PAT O'CONNOR FILM

DANCING AT LUGHNASA

A young boy tells the story of growing up in a fatherless home with his unmarried mother and four spinster aunts in 1930's Ireland. Each of the five women, different from the other in temperament and capability, is the emotional support system, although at times reluctantly, for each other, with the eldest assuming the role of a 'somewhat meddling' overseer. But then into this comes an elderly brother, a priest too senile to perform hisclerical functions, who has "come home to die" after a lifetime in Africa; as well, there also arrives the boy's father, riding up on a motorcycle, only to announce that he's on his way to Spain to fight against Franco. Nevertheless, life goes on for the five sisters, although undeniably affected by the presence of the two men, they continue to cope as a close-knit unit... until something happens that disrupts the very fabric of that cohesiveness beyond repair. This 1998 movie stars Meryl Streep, Michael Gambon and Gerard McSorley.

DID YOU KNOW...
Original choices to star were Frances McDormand and Kate Winslet.

The play originally opened in Dublin, Ireland in 1990. It opened on Broadway in New York City, New York, USA on 11 October 1991 and closed on 25 October 1992 after 436 performances. The play also won a 1992 Tony award as best play.

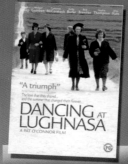

BRAY – DID YOU KNOW...?

County Wicklow · Ireland

braydidyouknow@gmail.com

PRESENTATION COLLEGE *(Part I of III)*

In 1920 The Presentation Brothers purchased Bray Head House from David Frame, which was once the home of the Putland family, who had the Putland Road built as a Famine Relief Scheme in 1862. The chosen site, with the mountains as a backdrop and the Irish Sea in the foreground, was intended to have an uplifting effect on future students. The following year, The Boys Roman Catholic Secondary School for primary and secondary education was established. The school was blessed and opened by the Archbishop of Dublin Dr. Byrne on September 5, 1921. It was Edmund Ignatius Rice who founded the order of the Presentation Brothers – incidentally he also founded the Irish Christian Brothers. Blessed Edmund Rice had given up his personal property and eminent status in society to found religious communities of Brothers dedicated to the education of the young. From the beginning, the Brothers, inspired by their founder, cultivated in the College an atmosphere of love, friendship, trust and loyalty.

At that time of opening the new school, there were only 52 boys registered on the school roll, but over the next couple of years the amount of students entering the school was to increase so much, more space was obviously required. So in 1924 the old stables at the rear of Bray Head House were completely renovated into a new schoolhouse.

The building, though in a dilapidated condition, still stands here today.

to be continued...

Right: Bray Head House in 1912, when it was home of Charles Putland and family;
Top right: The Christian Brothers outside their new school in 1920;
Bottom right: The school as it was in 1921.

BRAY – DID YOU KNOW...?

County Wicklow · Ireland

braydidyouknow@gmail.com

THE PRESENTATION COLLEGE *(Part II of III)*

The gates and lodge in 1947.

A new wing of the school was added adjacent to the house in 1956, which consisted of an assembly hall and extra classrooms. The number of pupils on the roll was then 350. The third extension in 1970 provided the new college with an indoor heated swimming pool and new sports fields. The swimming pool held regular swimming classes and was opened to the public in the evenings and weekends. Many will remember buying their chips from the canteen / shop upstairs before leaving the swimming pool in the evening!

By now, the amount of students on the roll books had risen to 700 boys – and rising. So, in 1972 a brand new school was built, including many more classrooms and facilities. In the late 1980s, the primary school – the wing which was built in 1956 – closed its doors, the building is now home to the Bray Adult Education Centre.

By the new millennium there had literally been thousands of boys that came through the gates of 'Pres' to complete their secondary school education. Some famous and very well known students were educated at Presentation College including Reggie Corrigan (below right), the former Irish rugby international and Leinster Captain; RTÉ sports pundit and former Olympic swimmer Gary O'Toole; Darren Randolph, goalkeeper for Motherwell F.C.; Seamus Costello (below left), Irish republican political activist; Chief Executive of Aer Lingus Gary Cullen; Pat Byrne, former Cityjet Chief Executive; Chairman of Bord Failte Mark Mortell and the infamous Sean FitzPatrick, the banker associated with Anglo Irish Bank.

But by now portions of the college built in the early 1970s were out of date, beginning to decay, some parts were even starting to crumble and the town itself was getting bigger, with new estates popping up here and there. So, yet again, a new school would be required.

to be continued...

The new wing (looking east) during construction in 1955.

© Bray - Did You Know 2012

PRESENTATION COLLEGE *(Part III of III)*

But 2003 spelt the end of an era for the Presentation College as the last remaining resident Christian Brother left the premises. In 2005 good news was received the Presentation College was to be granted funding for the construction of a new modern school building. However even though the Department of Education withheld payment until 2008, the College was given permission to start construction on the new school in January 2009, and construction on the new €7 million school was complete in time for the new school year in September 2011.

However, there was some nostalgia being felt as the bulldozers arrived to demolish the old 1970s school – including what was the old swimming pool area – in July 2011, which for many a student, past pupil and teacher alike held many memories – as it did for many people of Bray.

Today, the school have their own website at www.presbray.com or if you're a past pupil, you can check out www.presbrayppu.com. The new state of the art building includes a new sports hall, computer room, woodwork room and the outdoor facilities include a floodlit grass rugby field, astro turf soccer pitch, a basketball court, and several other playing fields. Curricular studies include German, physics, biology, chemistry, art and technical graphics.

To say that Presentation College has come on leaps and bounds since its humble beginnings back in 1920 is an understatement, as there are currently over 600 students on the roll books at the new-look College. When Edmund Ignatius Rice founded the school back then, he probably never thought that the school would evolve into such a major educational institution as it is today, so one can be pretty sure that it is a very proud Edmund Ignatius Rice that is looking down at the school today.

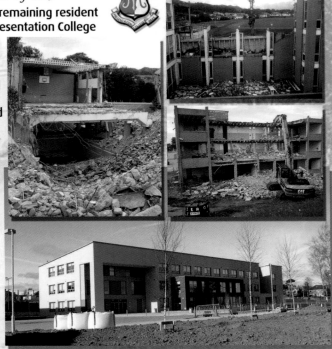

Top: Three photos of the demolition of the old school including the old sports room and swimming pool. Above: The new Pres school.

Bray - Did You Know...?

County Wicklow · Ireland

braydidyouknow@gmail.com

POSTCARDS FROM BRAY

Town Hall.   Bray.

The Town Hall & Market Place was built by Lord Brabazon between 1882 and 1883 on the site of the old 'Pound' at the top of Bray Main Street. It was designed by Thomas Newenham Deane and Son (formed 1878), leading architects of the day, however, Brabazon also got personally involved as evidence is plain to see on the building that Lord Brabazon was also trying to enhance his own image in the town, by reflecting his power and station.

154

BRAY - DID YOU KNOW...?

County Wicklow · Ireland

braydidyouknow@gmail.com

Those Forgotten Sounds of our Town (Part I of III)

Over the past few decades the town of Bray has expanded and with this some of the old and familiar sounds of the town have disappeared or are disappearing.

One of the first sounds a visitor coming to Bray would have heard was the cry *"Herald or Press"* by the newspaper seller Dan Reilly, better known as 'Chicken' Reilly on the Royal Corner at the Quinsboro Road. A full symphony of sounds have disappeared in the Railway Station including all the sounds associated with steam trains. The firm click as the white level crossing gates closed, the dropping of the railway signal and the line side signal wires snapping into place. The gush of water from the water tower. The shunting and coupling of the goods and commuter trains in the station and the goods yard.

When a train was about to depart Bray Station one could hear the loud bang of the train doors and the blow of the guard's whistle. The gentle hum of the diesel trains as they were left running when they were not in use either at the siding at Royal Marine Tce. or behind Fitzwilliam Tce.

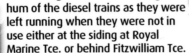

The railway goods yard had its own sounds, the moving of crates, barrels etc. and the loading of them on the horse and dray for delivery around the town. Going down the Albert Walk towards the seafront the call of the numbers from Mick's Pongo and the reply "House" was a familiar sound to residents and visitors alike. The projection box of the Roxy Cinema was just overhead and if the projection room door was open you would have sound without picture.

The clip clop of the horses belonging to Jarveys on the seafront included William Dodd of Diamond Terrace and Terry Kenny of Boghall and the Gaskin family of Dublin Road. During the summer months the Guinness Mechanical Clock would be located near the main bandstand. On each quarter of the hour some musical character would play a tune and then disappear with a full fanfare on the hour. The tannoy on the seafront announcing that some lost child was at the first aid post. The gentle roar of the Scragg's buses as they took tourists on day trips around Dublin and Wicklow.

to be continued...

BRAY - DID YOU KNOW...?

County Wicklow · Ireland

braydidyouknow@gmail.com

Those Forgotten Sounds of our Town (Part II of III)

One sound that will ever be associated with Sundays on Bray Seafront will be the sound of Michael O'Hehir's commentary on Gaelic football and hurling games as day trippers gathered around their transmitters to listen to their favourite match.

On Sunday afternoons a band would play on the seafront bandstand, the Artane Boys Band or one of the many brass and reed bands from Dublin. The céile on the seafront on a Sunday night when many hundreds would gather to listen to traditional music and see Irish dancing performed.

The laughing sailor outside Dawson's Amusements and the sounds of the cries coming from the Ghost Trains at Hunt's or Dawson's Amusements. Other cries of enjoyment would come from the children as they experienced their first ride on the merry-go-round or stood in front of one of the mirrors at the Hall of Mirror's at Dawson's Amusements.

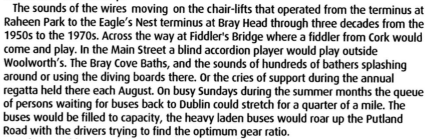

The churning of the sea by the paddleboats as some persons started their half hour journey into the unknown. The whistle of the paddleboat owners telling the would-be sailors their time was up.

The sounds of the wires moving on the chair-lifts that operated from the terminus at Raheen Park to the Eagle's Nest terminus at Bray Head through three decades from the 1950s to the 1970s. Across the way at Fiddler's Bridge where a fiddler from Cork would come and play. In the Main Street a blind accordion player would play outside Woolworth's. The Bray Cove Baths, and the sounds of hundreds of bathers splashing around or using the diving boards there. Or the cries of support during the annual regatta held there each August. On busy Sundays during the summer months the queue of persons waiting for buses back to Dublin could stretch for a quarter of a mile. The buses would be filled to capacity, the heavy laden buses would roar up the Putland Road with the drivers trying to find the optimum gear ratio.

When World War II ended the war-time air raid siren located behind the Town Hall and Fire Station was used to call out the firemen. In the early days after The Emergency when the siren was activated to call out the firemen on a call, UK visitors would enquire where the air raid shelter was located.

to be continued...

BRAY - DID YOU KNOW...?

County Wicklow · Ireland

braydidyouknow@gmail.com

Those Forgotten Sounds of our Town (Part III of III)

When local elections took place the candidates would call out their supporters using a tannoy attached to a car. This was also used when a circus would come to town or Mrs McNiece letting everyone know a play was taking place in the Little Flower Hall. She used to emphasize the word 'Little' in Little Flower Hall.

There were also the sounds of the battery operated vans that provided door to door services for bread, milk and laundry. These included Premier Dairies, Johnston Mooney & O'Brien, Kennedy's Bread and Dartry Laundry. All now long gone.

Story courtesy of Brian White

Today there are still sounds around the town, but not like the old sounds that a lot of us became familiar with. There are no newspaper sellers at the corner, no sounds of horses' hoves, no day trippers around their transistors, no brass bands on the bandstand, no laughing sailor or Ghost Trains, no Dawson's Amusements, no paddleboats, no chairlifts, no fiddler or accordian players, no Woolworth's, and no terminus at the boathouse.

Yes, today there are different sounds. There are very few places you can go to in our town now without hearing the roar of cars, buses, trucks and motorcycles passing. The sounds of ambulances or other sirens are hardly a cause for concern anymore. The daily screech of low-flying passenger jets and helicopters in our skies is common now. Mobile phones seem to be an essential part of our lives today – and nearly everbody has one. But some of us still have the priceless memories – the memories of those forgotten sounds of our town.

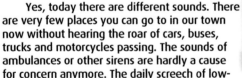

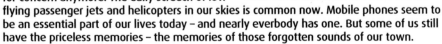

© Bray - Did You Know 2012

157

The Meath Road (so called after the Meath family of Killruddery House) runs from the Putland Road at the foot of Bray Head to Albert Avenue, which is at the northern end. But the Meath Road was actually much longer than it is now, as the Adelaide Road was part of the Meath Road up until 1907.

Here there are two photos (far right) c. 1890 and two modern photos taken from nearly the exact same place.

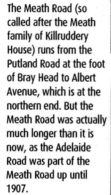

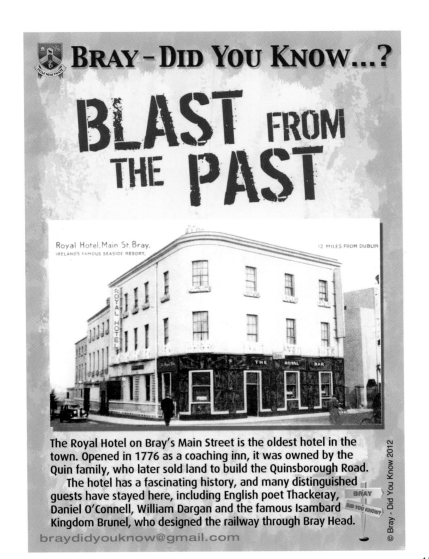

BRAY - DID YOU KNOW...?

BLAST FROM THE PAST

Royal Hotel, Main St. Bray.
IRELAND'S FAMOUS SEASIDE RESORT.

12 MILES FROM DUBLIN

The Royal Hotel on Bray's Main Street is the oldest hotel in the town. Opened in 1776 as a coaching inn, it was owned by the Quin family, who later sold land to build the Quinsborough Road.
The hotel has a fascinating history, and many distinguished guests have stayed here, including English poet Thackeray, Daniel O'Connell, William Dargan and the famous Isambard Kingdom Brunel, who designed the railway through Bray Head.

braydidyouknow@gmail.com

© Bray - Did You Know 2012

The Royal Hotel

A photo of the Royal Hotel taken from a 1970s brochure.

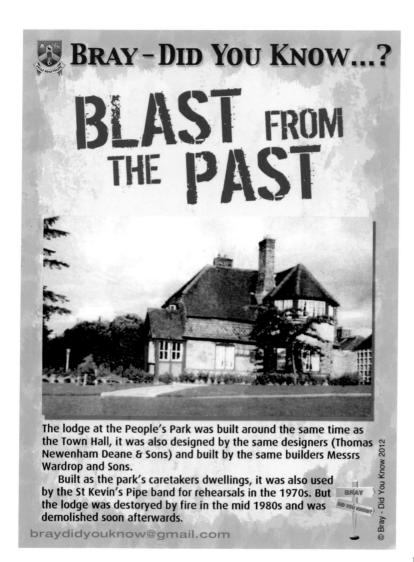

BRAY – DID YOU KNOW...?

BLAST FROM THE PAST

The lodge at the People's Park was built around the same time as the Town Hall, it was also designed by the same designers (Thomas Newenham Deane & Sons) and built by the same builders Messrs Wardrop and Sons.

Built as the park's caretakers dwellings, it was also used by the St Kevin's Pipe band for rehearsals in the 1970s. But the lodge was destoryed by fire in the mid 1980s and was demolished soon afterwards.

braydidyouknow@gmail.com

© Bray - Did You Know 2012

The Park Lodge

The Park Lodge from Bray Bridge looking west.

BRAY - DID YOU KNOW...?

County Wicklow · Ireland

braydidyouknow@gmail.com

THE FEVER (PART 1 OF 2)

A word that would strike fear into the entire population in Victorian times. It was not only hunger that was responsible for so many deaths in Ireland during that period. Death came in another and perhaps more fearsome guise, and was no respecter of class or circumstance, a death from which there was little chance of escape, even for those whose appetites were always satisfied. A word that struck terror and despair into our community, CHOLERA. It was to stalk the land laying its cold hand on many and leading them to their graves in the prime of their lives.

Bray was not to escape the terrible disease that was to present an appalling spectacle of misery and sorrow by the continuous flow of sad funeral processions to St. Peter's, St. Paul's, Old Connacht and Kilmacanogue cemeteries throughout many decades of the nineteenth century.

At the same time typhoid was rampant and was confused with cholera, but to most of Bray's population there was no difference, they described the scourge of the grim reaper as simply, 'the fever'. The spread of the contagion was swift because of the condition in which the people had to live. Contemporary medical notes read:

The great want of house accommodation for the lower classes is a formidable obstruction to sanitary measures. The damp state of the weather is favourable to the development of the scourge.

to be continued...

Top left: St. Paul's cemetery off Bray's Main Street with many graves of cholera victims buried here and in Old Connaught's cemetery (left).

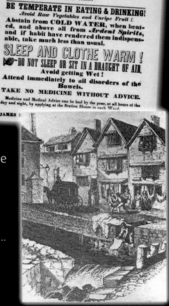

NOTICE.
PREVENTIVES OF
CHOLERA!
Published by order of the Sanitary Committee, under the sanction of the Medical Council.

BE TEMPERATE IN EATING & DRINKING!
Avoid Raw Vegetables and Unripe Fruit L.
Abstain from **COLD WATER**, when heated, and above all from *Ardent Spirits*, and if habit have rendered them indispensable, take much less than usual.

SLEEP AND CLOTHE WARM !
☞ **DO NOT SLEEP OR SIT IN A DRAUGHT OF AIR.**
Avoid getting Wet !
Attend immediately to all disorders of the Bowels.
TAKE NO MEDICINE WITHOUT ADVICE.

Medicine and Medical Advice can be had by the poor, at all hours of the day and night, by applying at the Station House in each Ward.

JAMES

THE FEVER (PART 2 OF 2)

Poor people's lives at the time were cheap and there was little pity or sympathy from authority for the bereaved. Medical advice at the time on how to combat the disease read: *As the great depression of the vital powers and the consequent coldness of the surface it is obvious that to rouse the system and restore the warmth of the surface of the body are the objects that require to be effected. A vapour or hot air bath should be had recourse to if at hand, as this, however will probably but seldom be the case, put the patient into a hot bed and apply a large hot mustard poultice over the pit of the stomach. Then let a blanket wrung out of a tub full of boiling water, as hot and dry as possible, be laid over his body. Put bottles of hot water; bags of hot sand or hot bricks or tiles wrapped in flannel into the bed.* This advice ends with the consoling words *"Do not fear catching the complaint yourself. Your very exertions will be the best and surest means of preventing your being attacked."*

Alas, these cures and assurances were of no benefit to one of the most prominent of Bray's doctors, Dr. Christopher Thompson, who helped combat the spread of infection; he himself caught the fever from his patients and his memorial in front of the Royal Hotel on the Main Street reads:

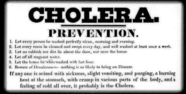

CHOLERA.

PREVENTION.

1. Let every person be washed perfectly clean, morning and evening.
2. Let every room be cleaned and swept every day, and well washed at least once a week.
3. Let no rubbish nor dirt lie about the door, nor near the house.
4. Let off all stagnant water.
5. Let the house be whitewashed with hot lime.
6. Beware of Drunkenness— nothing is so likely to bring on Disease.

If any one is seized with sickness, slight vomiting, and purging, a burning heat at the stomach, with cramp in various parts of the body, and a feeling of cold all over, it probably is the Cholera.

This Fountain Is Erected
To The Memory Of
Christopher Thompson
FFCSI
Who Died Dec. 16. 1876
In Testimony Of His Worth

Dr. Thompson's remains lie just across the road in St. Paul's churchyard with many of his patients. It was the sanitary conditions that prevailed that caused the spread of the disease; and Bray was in an appalling condition in the 19th century because of lack of toilets, sewers and the un-hygienic disposal of waste. It was a veritable breeding ground for 'the fever'. The Urban Sanitary Authority of Bray was established to combat the causes, and they were given power to have houses levelled if they found it necessary. Many of the small cottages were rented and it was the landlords who were responsible for the awful state in which the poor had to live.

Ascaill Shean-Channacht
OLD CONNAUGHT AVENUE

Modern photographs (left and below left) of Old Connaught Avenue and a photo of the village back in 1950 (below). Old Connaught was once known as *Connagh* or *Konagh* and was a small independent village and parish.

Note the old water pump, which is now gone on the left-hand side of the road in the photo below.

The photo on the right was taken in c. 1912, the photo above had to wait about one hundred years later. Much of the seating is long gone from our Promenade now, mainly due to the many storms which took their toll over the years. The Promenade lighting then was by gas, and the lamps were only placed at the pathways off the Promenade. Today the new state of the art lighting is every few hundred feet along the prom, although many would would say they are far from suitable for a Victorian Promenade.

164

BRAY – DID YOU KNOW...?

County Wicklow · Ireland

braydidyouknow@gmail.com

Memories of Bygone Days...

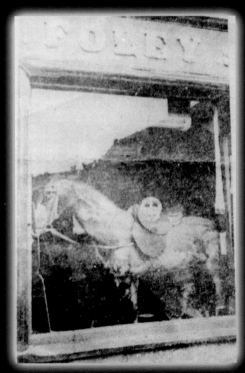

Joe and Bob Foley, of Foley's Saddlers stand proudly at the door of their shop in Castle Street, Little Bray.

Foley's were very well known in the equestrian fraternity throughout County Wicklow.

The shop, now incorporated into a large opticians business opposite Castle Street Shopping Centre, will be remembered mostly for the full sized stuffed pony in the window - not many passed by without casting a curious glance at the creature in the front window of Foley's Saddlers.

BRAY – DID YOU KNOW...?

County Wicklow · Ireland

braydidyouknow@gmail.com

MADE IN BRAY

ARDMORE STUDIOS IRELAND

The Webster Boy

The Webster Boy is a case of a weak script and strong actors combining for a mediocre tale about a love triangle. John Cassavetes is Vance Miller, an American with a serious gambling addiction who is just through with serving time and ready to finally go back to England. His objective is to find his long-lost love Margaret (Elizabeth Sellars) and try to start life over with her. When he does find Elizabeth, she is happily married to Paul (David Farrar) and is the mother of fourteen-year-old Jimmy (Richard Sullivan). As Vance upsets the apple cart trying to win Elizabeth away, young Jimmy faces taunts at school and a sadistic school master – and doubts as to who his real father might be.
Released in 1962, this black and white movie starred Richard O'Sullivan, John Cassavetes and Elizabeth Sellars. Directed by Don Chaffey.

DID YOU KNOW...
A 16mm print of this film has been preserved by the Limerick Film Archive in County Clare.

Director Don Chaffey is chiefly known for his fantasy productions, which include *Jason and the Argonauts* (1963), *The Three Lives of Thomasina* (1964), *One Million Years B.C.* (1966), *The Viking Queen* (1967), *Creatures the World Forgot* (1970), *Pete's Dragon* (1977), and *C.H.O.M.P.S* (1979), his final feature film. Chaffey also directed numerous British television series episodes, including several for The Prisoner, Danger Man, and The Avengers.

BRAY - DID YOU KNOW...?

County Wicklow · Ireland

braydidyouknow@gmail.com

POSTCARDS FROM BRAY

Bathing Strand, Bray

Originally used for practice by the volunteer Rocket Lifesaving Crew (who were based at the Coastguard Station) during the last quarter of the 19th Century, the Cove was known locally as the 'Rocket Bank'. But in the late 1890s, local fisherman Bart Naylor changed the Cove forever, as he leased the Cove from the Town Commissioners and built bathing boxes and a small pier. Over the next sixty years 'Naylor's Cove' would become a massive attraction with locals and tourists.

A train arrives at the Cove platform stop, which was located at the bridge.

The Town Hall & Market House (Part I of III)

Bray Town Hall and market house is prominently situated at the top end of the Main Street in Bray where the Main Street forks off to the Vevay Road and Killarney Road. Built in Tudor Revival style by Messrs Wardrop and Sons, it was commissioned by the 11th Earl of Meath's son and heir, Reginald Brabazon (1841-1929), Lord Ardee, who had lived abroad, and who seems to have been anxious to show interest in the town where his father was lord of the manor and the main ground landlord.

He wrote to the Bray town Commissioners in 1879 offering to erect a covered market house – as Bray had not had a market house since the demolition forty years earlier of one near Bray Bridge – and lease it to the Commissioners. But costs spiraled from the original £2,720 tendered in 1879 to a final total of £6,359, extras such as the clock added £1,000 more.

The design was by (Sir) Thomas Newenham Deane (1827-99) and Thomas Manly Deane (1851-1932) of the partnership of Thomas Newenham Deane and Son (formed 1878), leading architects of the day. Reginald Brabazon also got personally involved in the design of the building – as can be seen inside and outside of the building.

The construction is mainly of locally-made red brick, with timber framing projecting first floor bays and gables. The pitched roof is tiled and the two-storey portion facing the Main Street is surmounted by a tall copper-clad fleche complete with clock. Wrought iron gates on the west side and in the north porch carry the date 1881, although the building was largely built in 1882-3.

Perhaps the most impressive view of the Town Hall is from the side. From here it is possible to imagine the original busy market area, 62 feet long by 50 feet wide, with its arcades open to the street.

to be continued...

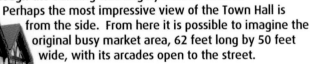

Left: The Town Hall viewed from its western side.
Top: Reginald Brabazon - the 11th Earl of Meath's son and heir who had the Town Hall built in 1882.

The Town Hall & Market House (Part II of III)

Some locals aptly called the building the 'Market House' and indeed this is what the ground floor was used for. A central aisle, at ground level, cut through the length of the building facilitated horse-carts (trucks in later years) to enter directly and unload their produce on the raised floor, right and left – this is where you now stand to order in the restaurant currently occupying the building.

But the Town Hall market was held once a week, everything from livestock, poultry, vegetables, straw and hay was sold. The farmers and their produce arrived from 6am and to facilitate them, the drovers, cart drivers and their helpers, the pubs in the Town Hall area had special opening licences. But by 8am business was up and running, and the day ahead was always going to be a busy one.

Who traffic here beware no strife ensue
In all your dealings be ye just and true
Let [justice] strictly in the scale be weighed
So shall ye call God's blessing on your trade.

The market house was closed in the mid 1940s, but the Town Hall's other major role continues. From the outset the Town Hall's council chamber was used by the Town Commissioners (later to become Bray & Urban District Council), while the adjacent upstairs office became the hub of local authority administration, making it the centre of much heated debate and discourse over the years!

The upper floor, reached by a stone staircase at the east side and with an open timber roof and oak chimney-pieces with carved panels, was always intended to serve as Bray's council chamber, originally for meetings of the Town Commissioners and today for Bray Town Council, it was also the venue for many historical events including a meeting to form an interim Civic Police Force when the Royal Irish Constabulary left Bray in 1921 and the founding meeting of the Bray & District Trade Union on 1 April 1917. It was also regularly used for local functions and dances. *to be continued...*

Top: A fine photo of the Town hall c. 1890.
Middle: A view of the town under the shadow of the Town Hall c. 1900.

Top right: Some of the stained-glass panels displaying the arms of the Brabazons and their wives.
Middle: The mock Tudor inscription in the south porch.

Bray – Did You Know...?

County Wicklow · Ireland

braydidyouknow@gmail.com

The Town Hall & Market House (Part III of III)

Just inside the front gate of the Town Hall (to the left) there was a door though which a stairs led to a basement apartment. This was the caretaker's living quarters, which included a living room and kitchenette. Another set of stairs led upwards where there were two bedrooms and a living room which boasted a coal fire that was the envy of many a visitor on a cold winter's night.

But evidence is plain to see on the building that Lord Brabazon was also trying to enhance his own image in the town, by reflecting his power and station. Thirty stained-glass panels displaying the arms of the Brabazons and their wives from Norman times onwards are incorporated in the windows. A specially carved fireplace and outside, the north front also has relief carvings of their coats of arms on the gables, while the drinking fountain is crowned by a wyvern, a mythological winged dragon from the Brabazon coat of arms. Over the years, this area directly in front of the Town Hall was used for political rallies and protests, none of which were timid affairs. The first meeting of the Town Commissioners in their new chamber was held in 1884. And the Town Hall had a rejuvenating effect on what was then a poor part of Bray, drawing business up Main Street and leading to the replacement of old thatched cabins by good houses.

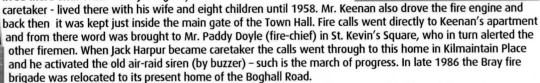

The Town Hall also had its resident caretakers, Mr. Bailey and his wife lived there until 1922. Then John (Jack) Keenan - the last resident caretaker - lived there with his wife and eight children until 1958. Mr. Keenan also drove the fire engine and back then it was kept just inside the main gate of the Town Hall. Fire calls went directly to Keenan's apartment and from there word was brought to Mr. Paddy Doyle (fire-chief) in St. Kevin's Square, who in turn alerted the other firemen. When Jack Harpur became caretaker the calls went through to this home in Kilmaintain Place and he activated the old air-raid siren (by buzzer) – such is the march of progress. In late 1986 the Bray fire brigade was relocated to its present home of the Boghall Road.

The building underwent change in the 1970s when the arcade openings were filled in and the market space became municipal offices. In 1991, after major refurbishment, the ground floor was converted into a high-ceilinged restaurant called the 'House of James Centre Restaurant' and in 1997 this was taken over by the *McDonald's* food chain. It could be argued that this change of use - controversial at the time - has again attracted extra business to the area and, indeed, that the fast-food company is today's inheritor of a long tradition on this site of feeding the people of Bray. After all, when it was opened the market house was said to have 'a large and commodious coffee-stall' which Lord Brabazon held franchise to.

MAIN STREET

Hallmark, or *Occassions*, is now at no. 101 on the Main Street in Bray. Situated near the Church of the Most Holy Redeemer, the greeting card and gift shop looked a lot different when Mr. Begley and Mr. Meehan ran their spirit merchant business from here up until 1899. But the premises wasn't long left vacant, as in 1900 James Carberry opened his fruit, vegetable and flower shop in no's. 101 and at 102 and was very successful for many years in the town of Bray.

Bóthar Bhaile Uí Chuínn
QUINNSBOROUGH ROAD

The Quinsborough Road in the early 1940s. The *Royal Cinema* on the left and next to it was *Mezza's Silver Lounge*. The Quinsborough Road had some great shops, including *Coyne's* and the wonderful smell of tobacco when you would walk by. *Tansey's* (still in business) were always busy and *Harvey's* sold fruit, veg, fresh fish and game. There was *Brown's* hardware where you could get tools, paints, gardening equipment and oils! *Taylor & Co.* quality butchers were there (the shop front still there today), *Tylers Shoes* were there and always had customers, and the *Northern Bank* was opposite the *Lido Café* who did a super bag of chips! And everyone must have tried a delicious fresh cream cake from *Johnston, Mooney & O'Brien's*...Ah, the good old days!

© Bray – Did You Know 2012

Bray's Bike Club

The Bray and District Motor Cycle Club was formed in the early fifties after a meeting in a shed in the yard of Meckins Pub on the Main Street by a bunch of enthusiasts. Amongst others present were John Inughman, Bill Clarke, Mick Reynolds, Kevin Meade and Jim Toal. It was decided to write a letter to the then *Evening Mail* newspaper stating the outlines of the club and inviting prospective members to an inaugural meeting a fortnight later. A venue on Quinsborough Road was selected and about thirty people turned up at the meeting.

A committee was formed and it was decided that the club would be a touring-only club providing for such things as Sunday outings, mystery runs, treasure hunts etc. Film shows were also organised showing various events such as the T.T. Races etc. These were usually held in the Little Flower Hall.

As time went on the club became affiliated to the Motor Cycle Union of Ireland and a decision was taken to organise a Motor Cycle Scramble in Bray.

Permission was obtained from the Earl of Meath and Bray's first motorcycle event went ahead on 16th May 1954. It was a huge success and on that bright sunny day crowds of people on foot, by car and of course motorcycles could be seen making their way to the venue. In later years other events were held in Fassaroe. The club then developed into a mainly sporting club which led to its demise in the late fifties or early sixties. No attempts were ever made to revive it.

Kevin Meade

Right: Programmes from the club's events;
Above: Members of the club meet at the Town Hall in 1956 before an outing.
Top: At the Town Hall in 1955, the photo includes: P. Meagher, Bill Clarke, John MCGovern, N. O'Keefe, J. Toal and Bill Kavanagh.

BRAY - DID YOU KNOW...?

County Wicklow · Ireland

braydidyouknow@gmail.com

The 'Thomas Ferguson'

The words 'Thomas Ferguson - Bray' appear on the stern of the brig that is photographed below. It is seen here beached on the shingle of the Dargle estuary, years before the harbour was constructed. This wooden vessel brought coal to Ireland from Whitehaven and Maryport and elsewhere in Scotland. Throughout the nineteenth century, several similar small craft were engaged at Bray in exporting grain and importing coal, slate and limestone.

The brig weighed 66 tons, having been built in 1857 in New Brunswick, Canada, by a master mariner named Thomas Fergusson (double 's'). It appears to have been acquired soon afterwards by one Mary Anne Menzies Oakes of Inverness. However, in 1862 it was registered at Dublin and, by 1863 at the latest, it was working out of Bray. In 1872, 'in excellent order, having within the last six months received extensive repair', the brig was put up for auction. Whether or not then sold, it subsequently belonged to one of Bray's leading merchants, Richard Cuthbert, and its crew rescued a man from the sea at Bray in 1880. On 25 September that year, the Irish Times reported how,

> On Monday night a man named John Murphy accidentally fell into the dock of Bray and had a narrow escape from drowning, there being nine feet of water in the river at the time. It would appear that Murphy, who is a very old man, was walking on this roadway, which is close to the dock and in a very dilapidated condition at present, owing to the place having been torn up for the purpose of removing some old gas-pipes, when he slipped and fell into the water. His cries attracted the attention of a railway fireman named Russell, who ran out of his residence, close by, with a hand towel, and threw the end of it to the drowning man, who succeeded in keeping hold of it until a boat came from the schooner Thomas Ferguson, belonging to Mr Cuthbert, which was lying in the dock at the time, the crew taking him ashore.

Alas, five years later, the crew of the brig itself were less fortunate. On 11 May 1885, carrying coal from Troon to Bray, the vessel was lost off Corsewell Point in Scotland.

The Thomas Feguson docked at the Compensatory Dock c. 1880 – years before the construction of the harbour. In the background (right) the International Hotel can be seen.

BRAY - DID YOU KNOW...?

County Wicklow · Ireland

braydidyouknow@gmail.com

The International Hotel (*Part I of IV*)

The International Hotel was originally built on land owned by Mr John Quin – who not only owned Quin's Hotel on Bray's Main Street, but also all the land running eastwards from the hotel to the sea - the railway station and Quinsborough Road were built on his land. The International hotel was owned by James Brennan, a Bray businessman who put much investment in the project, it was designed by architect E. O'Kelly and the first stone was erected on the 18th February 1861. However, Brennan died only a year later in 1862, his son-in-law Charles Dufresne eventually resumed proprietorship of the hotel and his son John Brennan inheriting house property.

The magnificent hotel was not only the largest hotel in Ireland when it opened for business on 31st May 1862, but it was considered one of the largest hotels in the British Isles...with its white eagle statues sitting proudly around the perimeter of the building, high up over its porch entrance and 250 magnificent rooms.

A c. 1890 photo of the International Hotel and some of the many carmen at the ranks waiting on customers - like taxis nowadays.

However, neither Dufresne or John Brennan were developers, and the International closed and changed hands three times in the first six years and at least once as a vacant premises – notably in 1900-1, rather than as a going concern. The hotel also fell into the hands of Edward Breslin – the original owner of the Marine Station Hotel – for a time. Records show that it was sold, again in 1875, was put up for sale once again in 1878 at £10,000 (half its building cost), but got no takers.

The International Hotel was described in 1869 as rising 'phoenix-like' from the ashes of decay. Most significantly, its rateable valuation, £455 in 1863, was reduced to £405 by 1870, £305 by 1881 and £260 by 1887. A list of visitors to the town in August 1900 showed only forty-three guests staying in the International Hotel – and this being a hotel with over 250 rooms.

to be continued...

A damaged photo of the hotel with the Royal Marine Hotel - across the railway - in the background.

The International Hotel *(Part II of IV)*

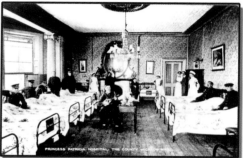

The Bethall family purchased the hotel in the early 1900s – incidentally they also owned the Bray Head Hotel and the Marine Station Hotel (situated beside the International on the seafront) – but in July 1915 the hotel was leased from the Bethall family by the British Red Cross and St. John's Ambulance Association and went under the name 'The Princess Patricia Hospital for Wounded Soldiers'. Initially it was used for the fitting of artificial limbs and then for convalescent cases from the Dublin hospitals. The soldiers would sometimes play tennis and even cricket tests were organised with the students of the Aravon School in the gardens at the rear of the hotel. It was not until 1919 that Frank Bethell resumed possession of the International again as a hotel.

But the hotel stood empty and neglected for long periods in the 1920s and early 1930s, and it was not until 1935 that it was reopened as an A.P. Friendship Holiday Association guest-house – not a hotel. Between 1939 and 1945 – during 'the emergency' - the hotel was occupied by the army,

THE BETHELL HOTELS, Ltd.

International Hotel, Bray.

.100 Rooms.   Splendid Situation.   Re-decorated
30 minutes by rail from Dublin.   **and**
   15 ,, ,, ,,   Kingstown.   Re-furnished.

EXCELLENT CUISINE AND WINES.

Terms from 7/6 per day.

and although the hotel was back in business as a hotel in the late 1940s – catering mainly for British visitors who wanted to get away from war-torn Britain and the austerity and rationing – the International was up against tough competition when it came to getting in the crowds. One of the main problems, that must must have always been a drawback in attracting visitors, was the proximity to the railway. Visitors staying on the east and south wings continually complained that they were being kept awake by the noise of the steam trains and shunting engines, added to by the merriment in the Arcadia ballroom immediately behind the hotel. Top entertainment spots including the famous Arcadia Ballroom, the Eagle's Nest Ballroom on Bray Head, the Maple Ballroom and Bar B at Woodbrook were attracting the crowds in huge numbers every weekend.

to be continued...

Clockwise from left: An early advertisement for the hotel; The International hotel re-opens after a vacant spell c. 1901; One of the wards at the Princess Patricia Hospital in c. 1918; Above: The soldiers and nurses watching a cricket game at the back of the hospital.

BRAY – DID YOU KNOW...?

County Wicklow · Ireland

braydidyouknow@gmail.com

The International Hotel (Part III of IV)

In the summer of 1947, English writer and broadcaster S.P.B. Mais (Petre Mais) visited Bray with her family and stayed in the International Hotel. Of her experience, Mais wrote: *"There was pandemonium, the reception desk, for it contained the only telephone in the building, one of the old-fashioned kind that you have to press firmly before you can hear what the speaker is saying. There was a continual running in and out of visitors and page-boys, and a mass of people surging round the reception-clerks asking for information. The friendly manager – who looked no more than nineteen – apologized for our rooms, and promised we would be moved later in our stay. We then climbed a wide staircase and entered and enormous bedroom which looked out on a blank wall. It was quite dark. There was no hot water. We were told that the hotel had only just been de-requisitioned and that they cannot install a hot-*

water system for some time to come. We are paying ten guineas a week each, and there's no hot water. ...This is unacceptable. There are two bars downstairs. These are so much occupied that it is difficult to force one's way to the counter."

The International Hotel had, in fact, only just reopened as a hotel; to restore it to its original function after some thirty years must have required considerable effort. Although the hotel's own barber shop was always doing a good business and the well known 'Round Bar' was always a favourite haunt for couples to have a drink before going on to somewhere to dance or back to Dublin on the last train. The cabaret shows did a lot better for the International in the 1950s and 1960s – and some big names were advertised on the posters outside, and it looked like the crowds were coming back to the International Hotel. But fate had other plans for the hotel...

to be continued...

Top left: One of the bars in the hotel in 1970; Below left: An aerial photo of the International Hotel in the 1940s. Top right: A poster from 19 March, 1974 advertising a function at the hotel - just four months before it was gutted.

The International Hotel *(Part IV of IV)*

One summer's night in July 1974 was to spell doom for the great hotel. Garda Dan Quill was on patrol on the Quinsborough Road that night and saw black smoke coming out of some of the chimneys. Thinking it was unusual for such smoke on a summer's night, he went into the hotel and was met by a man named O'Donovan

who was a commercial traveler and a guest in the hotel. Mr O'Donovan told Garda Quill that there was a 'small fire in the kitchen area' and that he had alerted the night porter. Garda Quill immediately went to the kitchen area and saw a deep fat fryer which was burning fiercely and flames were spreading up the wall and onto the ceiling and up into the first floor of the hotel. Shortly after, Garda Con Daly arrived on the scene, as did Garda Michael Barrett, Garda Tom Finn and Garda John Catles in a patrol car and they decided to evacuate the hotel of its guests and also rescued some goods from the premises.

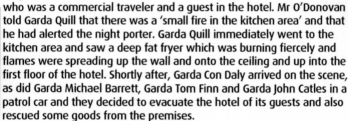

Fire brigade units from Bray, Greystones, Wicklow, Rathdrum, Dun Laoghaire and even Tara Street attended the fire. Water from the Dargle River had to be pumped up by joining hoses to help extinguish the fire, as water levels in the mains were low – some fire units were still at the scene the next evening. However, there was a lot of controversy about the fire after and how it started, local rumour had it that the fire was purposely set for insurance purposes.

The white eagle statues are now long gone. Shortly after the building was demolished and for many years after the site lay vacant. Today, a bowling alley is on the site – hardly an equal substitute for such a beautiful building that once was Bray's International Hotel.

Left (top & middle): The International on fire in 1974; Bottom left: The skeleton remains of the building after the fire; Right (top & middle): The demolition of the International Hotel after the fire; Bottom right: The Bray Gardai who helped in the removal of visitors and goods from the hotel, Sgt. Michael Barrett, Gardai Michael Mannion, Con Daly and John Catles.

BRAY - DID YOU KNOW...?

County Wicklow · Ireland

braydidyouknow@gmail.com

POSTCARDS FROM BRAY

Cliff Walk, Bray Head.

Bray Head Co. Wicklow.

The D.W.W. Railway Company built the Cliff Walk at the same time as the construction of the Railway, but it was not until 1869 that it opened to Greystones, originally called 'The Railway Walk'. The part of the trail from 'Fiddlers Bridge' to Lord Meath's gate remained the property of the Railway Company, the gate remained locked for one day a year.

POSTCARDS FROM BRAY

The Esplanade, Lawns and Head, Bray, Co. Wicklow.

Colour Photo by John Hinde, F.R.P.S.

A classic John Hinde postard (c. 1960) captures the Bray Seafront during its last decade as one of Ireland's top seaside resorts.

BRAY - DID YOU KNOW...?

County Wicklow · Ireland

braydidyouknow@gmail.com

Right: A photo taken c. 1965 at the Town Hall looking down the Main Street. The troughs at the wyvern were later covered.

Below: Thanks to Jim Sloan who sent us in this great photo taken on the chair-lifts at Bray Head in 1963, while Jim was holidaying in Bray with his family. Note the car park at the base of the head has not been built yet.

our transport of yesterday

One of Scraggs's coaches full of day trippers on an outing in Wicklow. Scraggs's had their large garage premises on the Main Street in Bray - where 'Winstons' shop was situated.

Joe Johnson with Pony 'Dolly' and trap for hire outside the old Bray Baths on the esplanade in 1960 - Scraggs's bus in the background.

John Quin's (of Quin's Hotel, Bray) Kingstown & Bray Motor Service bus at the 'Pavilion Gardens' (Dún Laoghaire) in 1907.

This was the Bray - Enniskerry Bus back in c.1890. Pictured here at Bray Railway Station collecting passengers before leaving for the village a few miles west of Bray.

The 84 (from Dublin) just after pulling in at the Railway Station terminus at Bray.

BRAY – DID YOU KNOW...?

BLAST FROM THE PAST

It's 1983 (left) and the shop behind the 45A is Gaffney's, King's butcher shop is centre and then the pork butchers Caprani's - hard to believe all three businesses are gone now - King's and Caprani's buildings are demolished too.

Looking down the Main Street, (right) The Royal Hotel corner was demolished in 1982 and the new building is underway. Muffin's bakery, Hazletts electrical, Sasha's and Woolworth's who pulled out of Ireland in 1984.

braydidyouknow@gmail.com

The Main Street

The north end of Main Street and Royal Hotel c. 1919.

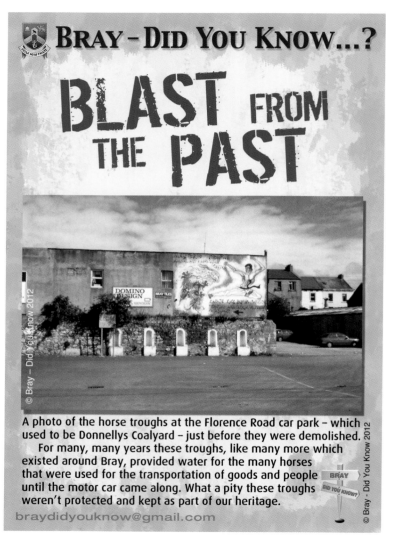

BRAY – DID YOU KNOW...?

BLAST FROM THE PAST

A photo of the horse troughs at the Florence Road car park – which used to be Donnellys Coalyard – just before they were demolished.
For many, many years these troughs, like many more which existed around Bray, provided water for the many horses that were used for the transportation of goods and people until the motor car came along. What a pity these troughs weren't protected and kept as part of our heritage.

braydidyouknow@gmail.com

© Bray – Did You Know 2012

The Horse Troughs

The horse troughs were demolished to make way for a car park.

Uncivil Days in Bray *(Part I of IV)*

Following a meeting in the Rotunda Gardens in November 1913 to organise the Irish Volunteers, a company was formed in Bray. The company won many recruits as a result of its part in the Kilcoole Gunrunning. On Easter Sunday 1916, Arthur Griffith called to Joe Kenny's house in Bray with a message from Eoin MacNeill cancelling the movement of volunteers that day. As a result of the confusion caused by the cancellation, the Bray Company took no part in the rising other than cutting telephone wires around the town.

The Bray Company was reorganized in 1917 when it became C. company of the 6th Battalion, Dublin Brigade. The company O.C. was Michael McGarry of Shankill. Weekly training was held in and around Pucks Castle, Ballycorus and target practice was held in Ballycorus quarry. From August 1918 onwards the company took part in numerous raids and attacks against Crown forces and on December 10th 1920, Section Leader Willie Owens was shot dead. Many raids for arms took place and weapons were dumped in the disused railway tunnel around Bray head. In an ambush on the military at Claffey's Grove, Crinken, three soldiers were injured. On 18th April 1921 the courthouse and R.I.C. barracks were attacked and as a result the Royal hotel was fortified and occupied by one hundred British soldiers *(see above)*.

Bray R.I.C. at their Bray barracks in 1916.

The following accounts are copied from contemporary sources:
Thursday 29 June 1922 - 4.00 a.m. - ATTEMPT TO BLOW UP BRIDGE *(Irish Independent, 30 June 1922)*
The inhabitants of Bray were startled at 4 a.m. on Thursday 29 June by the sound of a loud explosion. It was subsequently ascertained that an attempt had been made to blow up the bridge over the Dargle river between Little Bray and Bray [the bridge built in 1856]. The effort, however, was not wholly successful, but was sufficient to prevent traffic from passing. Cars coming into Bray from Dublin have to travel by the sea road [Ravenswell Road] and cross the bridge at the Harbour. The Irregulars, who hold the Police Barracks and Courthouse at Bray have made elaborate preparations for the defence of the building.

to be continued...

Uncivil Days in Bray *(Part II of IV)*

Saturday morning, 1 July 1922 - ALONG THE COAST *(Irish Times, 8 July 1922)*

The Irregulars evacuated Bray and Cabinteely without being attacked on Saturday. The evacuation took place at about noon, and caused the greatest excitement among the townsfolk. These forces had occupied the coast-guard station at Bray Head and the police barracks and courthouse at Dargle Bridge, and had strongly fortified them. At 9 a.m. on Saturday the men holding the post at the police barracks in Cabinteely, set fire to it, and left for Bray, the same was done at Enniskerry.

Before the evacuation of Bray the Irregulars made a round of the town's shops, and took away quantities of men's overcoats, suits, boots and other sorts of clothing, blankets, and cooking utensils. Food stuffs were also taken from provision shops. They seized the chars-a-banc belonging to the Wicklow Garage Company and other motor vehicles, 25 or 30 in all.

The reason for the exodus is not known, but it was evidently with a view to a concentration of forces, as

men were collected from all parts of East Wicklow and South County Dublin to the number of about 300. Before leaving they set fire to most of their quarters. They left Bray in some 25 or so motor vehicles, which had been commandeered from all directions. The coast-guard station was only roughly damaged where the Irregulars had been in occupation, but the courthouse and police barracks were fired. The courthouse was gutted and the roof fell in, but the barracks opposite suffered no very serious damage, although when the township fire brigade arrived, intent on putting out the fires, they were prevented by some persons from doing so. Three young men, who had been held prisoners by the Irregulars were released by them.

The courthouse was gutted before the Irregulars left Bray.

The Irish Free State army firing on the anti-treaty forces in the Four Courts. They finally surrendered on Friday 30 June, 1922.

to be continued...

Uncivil Days in Bray *(Part III of IV)*

Saturday afternoon - 1 July 1922.

[One day earlier, the anti-treaty O'Malley had escaped from the Four Courts.] We walked into Bray and found the barracks smoking but little damaged; our men had left for Blessington two hours before in such a hurry that they had not burnt their papers. What South Dublin had being doing since the attack on the Courts I could not imagine. A man walked over from the hotel door. He was the American gun-runner whom we had released a few hours before the attack on the Four Courts began.... I commandeered a motor-car and the two of us turned off the road near the Glen of the Downs, up by the Sugar Loaf mountains and crossed the Sally Gap [to Blessington]... next day the Tipperary column of seventy men came in a char-a-banc.

Monday 3 July 1922 - IN THE COUNTRY *(Irish Times, 8 July 1922)***.**

IRREGULARS RAIDING EXPEDITION

The Irregulars who cleared out of East Wicklow and South County Dublin area from Bray last Saturday, have since reappeared in different localities. On Monday night [3 July] they descended on Bray from the Enniskerry - Brittas direction in ten motor cars. Their first work was an attempt to complete the destruction of the police barracks that they had ineffectually fired before their evacuation of Bray.

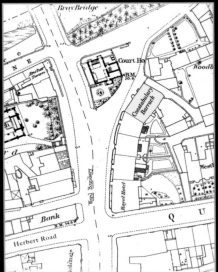

Police barracks facing the Courthouse. Detail from O.S. map of 1870.

Since last Saturday the barracks have been used by the civil town guard, organised by the parish priest, Father Bowden, for the protection of property. The guard got out of the building with their belongings, and the Irregulars poured in a quantity of petrol and set it alight. The attempt was, however, again a failure. Having set fire to the barracks, the Irregulars made a round of the shops and seized a quantity of foodstuffs. They then made off to Enniskerry, where a side of bacon and several pounds of butter were taken from Mr. Tallon's shop. They departed in the direction of Glencree for the mountains.

Co. Dublin concentration

The Bray contingent, having twice failed to burn the local barracks, left for Loughlinstown, where they were joined by a party from Cabinteely, and the combined forces moved off in commandeered motor cars and chars-a-bancs in the direction of the mountains. It is believed that their intention was to make for Blessington, where other irregular troops were stated to be concentrating. [Arklow and Gorey barracks were among others also reported to have been set on fire].

to be continued...

BRAY - DID YOU KNOW...?

County Wicklow · Ireland

braydidyouknow@gmail.com

Uncivil Days in Bray *(Part IV of IV)*

REPORT *(Irish Independent, 4 July 1922): Bands of irregulars are moving about in motors in the mountains between Enniskerry and Brittas, and it is presumed that they are the men who evacuated Bray. In the early hours of yesterday morning [Sun /Mon night] they swooped down on the town in ten motors and completely wrecked the police barracks. Since Saturday the building has been in the charge of the local guard formed by the Very Rev. Father Bowden, P.P.*

Tuesday 4 July 1922 - NEWS *(Freeman's Journal, 7 July): The body of Joseph Hamill, who was with the Irregulars in the Brittas district, was conveyed to Bray yesterday [i.e. Tuesday] and placed in the Church of the Most Holy Redeemer. He was a draper's assistant in Bray, and is stated to have been accidentally killed on service. It is rumoured that Mr. de Valera is with the Irregulars in that area.*

ALONG THE COAST *(Irish Times, 8 July): A detachment of the National troops was sent to Bray on Tuesday. Their arrival seems to have caused considerable satisfaction in the town, which was quiet throughout the night. Shots heard about the harbour on Tuesday night, thought to be fired by men in sympathy with the Irregulars.*

Wednesday 7 July 1922 - ALONG THE COAST *(Irish Times, 8 July): Some food stuffs and pots and pans, etc., left behind by the departing forces, have been distributed to the poor of Bray. The National troops, who now occupy Bray, have since recovered from houses in Little Bray a considerable quantity of goods which Irregulars had taken from Bray shops....[Local bridges reported damaged or mined and were impassable] Peace prevails in Bray since its evacuation by the Irregulars. The guard of citizens, numbering several hundred, formed on the initiative of the Very Rev. R.F. Bowden, PP, and representatives of all classes, has proved a complete success. Patrols are maintained throughout the night to prevent robbery. Business goes on as usual, and the damaged bridge has been repaired. Large numbers of country folk from outlying villages were emboldened to come into Bray for the monthly fair.*

Thursday 8 July 1922 - IRREGULAR LEADER TAKEN *(Freeman's Journal, 8 July):*
Andy MacDonnell, who was a leader of the Irregular forces and stationed at Bray Barracks, has been taken prisoner by the National forces ... in fighting around Blessington. He was in command of the large force of Irregulars who evacuated Bray on Saturday last after destroying the Courthouse and Barracks.

Top: The barracks at Rathfarnham was also destroyed by Irregular Forces. Above: Anti-Treaty IRA Troops - June 1922.

Sniping attacks by Irregulars on Bray Barracks are reported in the *Freeman's Journal & Irish Times* on 24/7/22 & 2/9/22.

Landslide De-Rails Wexford to Dublin Mail Train on Bray Head

The accident pictured occured in February 1923 when the mail train from Wexford, which was on route to Dublin, ran into a fall of rock just north of tunnel No. 1 and was derailed.

The fireman, Daniel O'Neill, was thrown from the footplate and rolled down the slope above the steep sea wall, but managed to hang on to be rescued.

However, as the photographs show, it was extreme luck that the Mail carriage did not go over the cliff edge, as after it derailed, it ended up only feet from the cliff edge and could have easily dragged the rest of the carriages over the edge into the sea.

Bray – Did You Know...?

County Wicklow · Ireland

braydidyouknow@gmail.com

The harbour (left) in 1979 - note the dilapidated state of the bridge across the river, and how much of the railings is missing - the bridge collapsed during a storm five years later.

Below: Bray Main Street during the mid 1970s, most of the shops and businesses are gone since, including Five Star Supermarket (after it became Winstons), Napier's shop, The Sugar Loaf Inn (now the Olde Bray Inn), and Woolworth's at the junction of the Florence Road (now Dubray Bookshop / City 2 clothing shop). The 70s...when buying your music you got a record, petrol was affordable and there was no parking problems and things were just always 'cool'!

Bray in the **70s**

The Mysterious Woman in Black *(Part I of II)*

In the years before the First World War there lived a couple at *Galtrim House*, Bray. Although it is no longer standing, Galtrim House was at that time an imposing mansion standing in its own large grounds at the rear of Quin's Hotel (now the Royal Hotel). By all accounts it was a large and well kept house with beautiful gardens, glass houses, an orchard, summer house and at one time even a cricket ground with a small ornamental pavilion, of course this was before Galtrim Park came to be built on its grounds.

Although he was a good deal older than she, they were a childless, but apparently devoted couple, known as a sociable pair who regularly entertained guests in their large house. They were also regarded as good employers by their staff, although it seems the kitchen maids considered Mrs. Lefroy a little grumpy. After many years of married bliss, Mr. Lefroy fell critically ill one day and though his wife was constantly at his side giving him the best medical care money could buy, his condition deteriorated with each passing day, until after two weeks the doctor warned her to expect the worst at anytime. She began to prepare for the ordeal to come. She went to McGuirk's Drapers and Outfitters on Bray's Main Street and had herself fitted out for a set of mourning clothes, collecting it the following day and bringing it home.

Unexpectedly her husband began to recover however, slowly but surely regaining his strength, so that by the following month he was able to get out of bed each day to sit by the fire in his room. On the first morning that he was able to go downstairs for breakfast, the morning post arrived, bringing with it a statement of account from McGuirks for the mourning suit. When he read of his wife's purchase, he could hardly believe his eyes. He immediately summoned the apparently eager-to-be widow and demanded from her an explanation. A quarrel ensued which developed into a dreadful fight lasting into the afternoon.

Eventually, the by now distraught wife stormed out of the room, went upstairs to put on the mourning clothes and then set out to taunt her husband. As she did so however, she missed her footing and fell headlong down the stairs. By the time she hit the ground floor, she was quite dead.

to be continued...

Left: Front of Galtrim House facing eastwards c.1912; Right: Galtrim House as seen from the south.

The Mysterious Woman in Black *(Part II of II)*

Soon after the funeral, various ghostly phenomena were reported around the house and grounds. At first it was only noises, the below stairs maids hearing the sound of crockery and cutlery being moved around the kitchen while at the same time the room became dreadfully cold. Then the parlour maid claimed to have heard a frightful and unearthly thumping sound on the stairs, a noise which was to be heard week after week as the poor dead mistress of the house met her ghastly end again and again.

Soon afterwards, the ghostly figure of a woman was seen around the grounds, appearing there on Autumn evenings all dressed in black, her dead eyes reflecting a gleam of fading daylight, her head hanging unnaturally to one side, her face motionless, chalk white and covered with a cold dew. She would by degrees become transparent and gradually vanish altogether.

These hauntings went on for many years and were experienced by many different people. I have spoken to three people who claim to have seen a

Galtrim House as flats in the 1970s.

woman in black around the grounds of Galtrim House at different periods over a long period of time. During the period of the building being the British Legion, the manager Mr Burke, who had lost an arm during the First World War, would never go upstairs alone in the evenings without someone accompanying him. While the building was flats during the 1970s/80s many of the tenants reported various mysterious sounds and strange sightings in the building.

The house is now demolished. Galtrim Court, a block of private apartments, stands on the spot now and nothing unusual had been witnessed there for many years until recently, when a man walking to work along Seapoint Road one summer's dawn reported seeing a woman in black mourning clothes. So it seems that the poor old soul still has not found her eternal rest.

As for the bereaved husband, he eventually regained his full health, and then married one of the parlour maids. He eventually sold Galtrim House and went to live in a new home on King Edward Road, which is just off the Killarney Road. *(Written by Henry Cairns)*

Galtrim Court stands on the site of the house today.

Tragedy at the Silver Bridge

On 30 August, 2010 Bray man Dermot Cranny was awarded the Red Cross Award of Merit recognising his bravery in a 1965 daring rescue operation. A former resident of the Dargle Road in Bray and now living in Glencormac, Dermot put his own life at risk when he waded into the cold River Dargle to attempt a rescue. It's almost 47 years ago when, nearly twelve hours after the car was taken from where it was parked on

Dermot Cranny pictured with his grandchildren and award.

Sunday night in Dublin, and eleven hours after it was heard crashing through the steel and stone parapet of the Silver Bridge on the N11 (Enniskerry junction), a Mini car was lifted with winches and grappling cables from the Dargle River about two miles south of Bray on 13 December, 1965. Gardai, sections of the Civil Defence and civilians had laboured all night to try to find the car which had disappeared beneath the muddy, flooded river. It was the following day when the car was located.

The then 27-year-old Dermot Cranny and his colleagues in the Bray branch of the Irish Red Cross were called out to help the Gardai in a search for the car with two occupants. It was a wet stormy night and the river was flooded with the water measuring between 5-6 metres in depth. A qualified Irish Red Cross Water Safety Instructor, Dermot entered the icy waters in his pyjamas with a rope tied around his waist to try to locate the car. But despite his best efforts however, the search had to be called off – the men's bodies were later found.

Left: Photographs of the incident at the Silver Bridge taken from the Wicklow People on Saturday 18 December, 1965

Captain Francis Leopold McClintock RN of Crowbank, Bray.

Captain John Franklin

Sir John Franklin was born in Lincolnshire in 1786. He joined the Royal Navy and served at the battles of Copenhagen in 1801 and Trafalgar in 1805. Franklin's ability as a surveyor was well recognised and in 1818 he went on a voyage of discovery to the Arctic under conditions of great hardship. Franklin and his men surveyed many thousand miles of North American Coastline as well as the Mackenzie River. Following this voyage Franklin was elected a fellow of the Royal Society after a further expedition to the Northern Territories in 1825 he was knighted and sent to Tasmania as Governor.

In 1845 Franklin, now 59 years old, was given command of an expedition to discover a North West Passage from the Atlantic to the Pacific Ocean. The expedition consisted of two ships the 'Terror' and The 'Erebus' with 129 officers and men, both ships were fitted with steam engines and propellers with supplies for three years including 2,900 books. They sailed on May the 19th from the Thames in London and after reaching Greenland moved out across Boffin Bay.

They were spotted by two whalers on July the 28th and were never seen again. A total of 32 separate expeditions were mounted to find Franklin and his men, and it was the Franklin search which finally resolved the question of where the North West Passage lay.

In 1858 the yacht 'Fox' under the command of Captain Francis Leopold McClintock of Crowbank, Herbert Road, Bray, was dispatched by Lady Franklin to search for Sir John. McClintock was born in Dundalk in 1819 and joined the Navy at the age of 12. A self-taught naturalist he took every opportunity to collect plant, animal and geological specimens. The 360 fossil specimens he collected are now housed in the Natural History Museum in Dublin. In June 1859 McClintock's expedition discovered two Cairns at the Victory Point containing the last reports left by the ill-fated Franklin expedition and confirming the death of Franklin.

Top: One of the Cairns discovered by McClintock; Left: Some of the items found in 1839 by McClintock's search party.

Killarney Wood off the Herbert Road, which is now Brook Wood School.

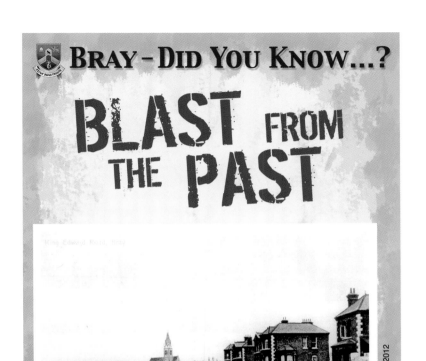

BLAST FROM THE PAST

Modest detached bungalows were being built on Florence Road and at the southern end of Meath Road during the 1920s and 1930s. More substantial houses were built on Bóthar Rí Eamoinn, or King Edward Road (above), which was named and opened on 6 October 1902.

braydidyouknow@gmail.com

© Bray - Did You Know 2012

BRAY DID YOU KNOW?

King Edward Road

The leafy King Edward Road as it is today.

The William Dargan Bridge

Under way: The new William Dargan bridge at the harbour in 1984.

BRAY – DID YOU KNOW...?

County Wicklow · Ireland

braydidyouknow@gmail.com

The 'Divil' of the Town Hall

The monument which occupies the civic space in front of the Town Hall is locally dubbed 'the statue of the divil'. However, it is in fact a fountain surmounted by a Wyvern holding a shield of the Brabazon crest. The wyvern comes from the Meath coat of arms and is a mythological creature whose upper half is a dragon and lower half a serpent or viper. Originally, the fountain was first designed as a base for a knight in armour representing a Meath antecedent. But in 1882, during the period of popular ill-feeling against Lord Brabazon from the locals, his architect T.M. Deane suggested to Lord Brabazon to replace the knight with the Virgin "who traditionally presided over fountains" and to ensure respect for the work of art when it was placed in its position. He added "I do not know whether you would think this was pandering to the R.C.'s...but we have as much right to the Virgin as they have". There is no recorded response, but subsequently the design incorporating the Wyvern, a Meath heraldic design, which was used around other parts of the Town Hall was adopted.

In the windows of the Council Chambers in the Town Hall itself, Wyverns can be seen in their correct colours of gold, with red wings and limbs collared and chained in gold. Years after, four water troughs were added around the sides of the base, but were recently covered in.

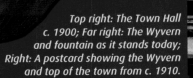

MAIN STREET FROM TOWN HALL. BRAY

Top right: The Town Hall c. 1900; Far right: The Wyvern and fountain as it stands today; Right: A postcard showing the Wyvern and top of the town from c. 1910.

The Move

Led by guitarist, singer and songwriter Roy Wood, The Move performed at The Arcadia in the mid 60s. They had some super hits such as 'NIght Of Fear', 'Flowers In The Rain', 'Fire Brigade' and 'Blackberry Way'.

They performed in Bray!

The Who

With hits like 'My Generation', 'Pinball Wizard', 'Substitute', 'Won't Get Fooled Again', 'Who Are You" and many more, the superband performed live at The Fillmore West Club in 1971.

Love Affair

The London based pop, soul, R&B group performed at The Arcadia for one night in the late 1960s. They had several UK Singles Chart Top 10 hits, including the No. 1 'Everlasting Love'.

Planxty

The Irish folk group played The Fillmore West Club in early 1972.

The Arcadia existed for many years in Bray on a large site opposite the Railway Station. During the 1960s many famous acts performed here, including The Hollies, Status Quo, Tom Jones, Manfred Mann, Rod Stewart and many more. In 1971 the name changed to The Fillmore West and for a year it continued to host many big acts until it closed in 1972.

© Bray - Did You Know 2012

BRAY • NOW AND THEN

County Wicklow · Ireland

braydidyouknow@gmail.com

Bóthar Bhaile Ui Chuínn
QUINNSBOROUGH ROAD

A wonderful photo c. 1893 of the Quinsborough Road looking west. Built on John Quin's land (owner of Quin's Hotel and after whom it was named) in 1854, the 'Forty-Foot Road' (original name) was laid out and opened by the Dublin and Wicklow Railway Company to coincide with the opening of the railway the same year. St. Andrew's Presbyterian Church on the left was built in 1858 and was extended on two occasions shortly after.

BRAY • NOW AND THEN

County Wicklow · Ireland

braydidyouknow@gmail.com

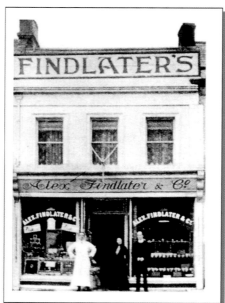

No. 17 Main Street, Bray, has a tradition of quality businesses at this premises since the late 18th century. When Thomas Gordon's druggist and general merchants shop closed in the first decade of the 19th century, Alex Findlater & Company – who had opened the Findlater Mountjoy Brewery in Dublin – took over the premises with his fine groceries and wine merchants business. Findlater's sold quality goods including chocolates, biscuits, canned goods, jams, polish, coffee and sugar etc, and even had their own extensive range of Findlater-brand teas. It was about 1930 when Richard Buckley took over No. 17 with a similar business as Findlater's, except he also sold Guinness stout, Bass ale and whiskeys as well as a butcher's business. Today McCabes shoe shop is at No. 17, and has been for many decades now.

Wicklow's Priest-Hunter *(Part I of II)*

The penal laws were instituted under William of Orange to retain land and power for the Protestant minority, while the majority of the Irish people struggled to survive. Catholics had no political rights, were barred from higher education, the professions and the purchase of land and forbidden to run schools. A Catholic gentleman's estate had to be split up between all his sons and could no longer be handed on intact.

An alternative for a Catholic and Irish education was found in the *Hedge Schools* which were held in secret, often in barns, caves or behind the hedges. These "schools" taught Irish history, tradition, music, and folk tales. Some also included classical training in Latin and Greek. While the majority of children received no schooling the children who did were mainly in Hedge Schools.

After 1703 the Catholic clergy had to be licensed by Dublin Castle; their official numbers were severely restricted. Unauthorised priests and supporters were liable to punishment if caught, while traditional religious practices, e.g., patterns and pilgrimages were forbidden. In June 1714 the high-sheriff and gentlemen of Wicklow stopped the St Kevin's pattern, Glendalough, by dispersing the crowd, destroying holy wells and tents and jailing a Catholic schoolmaster.

Catholic ownership of land in the county fell from about 50 per cent in 1641 to circa 14 per cent by 1688. This decline continued; the Catholic gentry families of Wicklow vanished, leaving only the Byrnes of Ballymanus, but friars and priests continued their work

However, it is debatable whether the penal laws were fully implemented, except at times of political unrest. Nevertheless, this legislation overshadowed the majority of the people during the early eighteenth century.

to be continued...

Clockwise from top left: An original copy of the Penal Laws; The hedge school teacher was greatly respected by the parents and was a welcome guest in their homes where he got the best bit to eat and the warmest corner to sit in; Priests and Bishops were punished and often hung for practicing the Catholic religion; A stone would usually be taken from a church ruin, and relocated to a rural area, with a simple cross carved on its top. Because the activity was illegal, the services were not scheduled and their occurrence was communicated verbally between parishioners.

BRAY - DID YOU KNOW...?

County Wicklow · Ireland

braydidyouknow@gmail.com

Wicklow's Priest-Hunter *(Part II of II)*

   Dublin Castle's reward for the arrest and conviction of unregistered clergy produced professional priest-hunters, who were hated by Catholics and despised by Protestants. From 1710 on, Edward Tyrrell, who had been educated as a Catholic on the continent, was a leading priest-hunter. He traveled the country looking for Catholic priests and bishops. Tyrrell was motivated by declining finances, informing the authorities of popish plots and Jacobite conspiracies, including the apparent discovery of a cardinal in Clonmel.

Dublin Castle directed magistrates to assist Tyrrell during his travels in Ireland, accompanied by a military escort. Tyrrell was working to enforce the 'Act to prevent the further Growth of Popery', commonly known as the 'Popery Act' or the 'Gavelkind Act', which was an Act the Parliament of Ireland passed in 1703.

   According to Bishop Donnelly, Tyrrell, posing as a Catholic, spied in Flemish colleges to sound out Fr. John Talbot, parish priest of Old Connaught. On his return to Ireland, Tyrrell was laid up in Fassaroe with a fever, before contacting the local magistrate, Richard Edwards, with his deposition. We do not know what, if any, action Edwards took.

   Tyrrell also tried to arrest Edward Byrne, the clandestine bishop of Dublin by organising raids on sympathisers' houses from Wicklow town in 1712. Local gentlemen considered Tyrrell a nuisance, while Dublin Castle began to lose faith in the expensive agent's wild reports. He was convicted of bigamy and executed on May 28, 1713 having been reprieved for fifteen days after his original execution date.

Mass in the Penal Days at St. Mullins, Co. Carlow

Left: Fassaroe Castle - where Tyrrell stayed while ill.
Right: Mass during the Penal days at St. Mullins in Co. Carlow.
Note the man on lookout on the left.

BRAY – DID YOU KNOW...?

County Wicklow · Ireland

braydidyouknow@gmail.com

Bray's Ale House Spies

About two centuries ago in Bray, the parishioners of the established church were empowered by an act of Parliament to appoint people (referred to as 'Spies') whose function was to inspect premises in Bray that sold beer, wines or spirits.

They scoured the whole Bray area and were entitled by law to forcefully remove any person found drinking in them at 'unreasonable hours'…

The job of the 'Spy' was to ensure, among other things, that no alcohol was sold on Sundays before four o' clock in the afternoon.

The trangressor, if caught, was fined and the money collected from the fine was distributed to the chosen charity of the 'Spy'.

These establishments were known as 'Dram Shops' or 'Tippling Houses', and there were quite a few of them around Bray back then.

BRAY • NOW AND THEN

County Wicklow • Ireland

A recent photo and a photo c. 1930 of the top of the Albert Walk, which is between the train station and Albert Avenue. Donnelly's tobacconist and hairdressing saloon was at no. 1, Wallace Brothers coal mercants had their office at no. 2 – their coal yards were at the harbour. At no. 3 among these wonderful little shops was Mannion's Café; one could not pass without smelling the sweet smelling aromas wafting from their quaint and comfortable premises.
Today no. 1 is no more, no. 2 is vacant, but Oli's Coffee House is at no. 3 carrying on the wonderful tradition of the wonderful cafés on the Albert Walk.

BRAY - DID YOU KNOW...?

County Wicklow · Ireland

braydidyouknow@gmail.com

POSTCARDS FROM BRAY

The 'White Coons' were formed by Clifford Essex in 1899, originally called the 'White Coons & Banjo Troupe', they played in Bray for many years, mostly performing on the small bandstand which was opposite the Esplanade Hotel and was mostly reserved for visiting variety shows.

BRAY - DID YOU KNOW...?

County Wicklow · Ireland

braydidyouknow@gmail.com

BRAY
DID YOU KNOW?

POSTCARDS FROM BRAY

Main Street, Bray, County Wicklow, Ireland.   ©21659

Bray Main Street in the mid to late 1960s. Note the amount of people shopping in the town. This was a time when Bray was buzzing and businesses did a roaring trade. No empty premises on Main Street then!

POSTCARDS FROM BRAY

I Picked
this
up at

BRAY

and Thought
of You!

BEST STOUT

BOTTLED BY
POLICHY L?
CORK
IRELAND

Something good inside you'll find
To bring the old place to your mind.   764

I'm taking this on for the
holidays only
AT BRAY.

The Brandy Hole *(Part I of II)*

The wild and lonely coast of Wicklow offered so many facilities for smuggling that the efforts of the Government were unable to accomplish more than barely to interrupt and at most delay the well-laid schemes of the contrabandists.

The usual plan adopted by smuggling vessels plying here was, under cover of night or misty weather, to send their contraband goods ashore in boats to the pre-concerted places of concealment on the coast, and then to sail openly with their legitimate cargo to Dublin or other port, and thus hoodwink the Revenue authorities. There can be little doubt, however, that corruption was rife among the Revenue and Customs officers at that period, and that they could, when necessary, look in the wrong direction.

The natural conformation of the coast around Bray Head lent itself readily to the adaptation of places of concealment, of which there were several, but the principal one was that known as *The Brandy Hole*, half a mile along the shore from where the road crosses the railway on the Head. Here was an immense cavern, with its entrance opening to the sea, and its many ramifications extending far in under the hill, affording ample accommodation for the cargoes of all the vessels plying their risky trade here. Into this great natural store-house, fully laden boats were able to make their way by the light of lanterns, and discharge their contents high and dry into the numerous receptacles prepared for them.

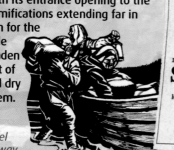

A SHIP HAS BEEN SIGHTED in this quarter ENGAGING IN THE UNLAWFUL ACT OF

SMUGGLING

whosoever can lay information leading to the capture of this ship or its crew will receive a reward of **£500**

From His Majesty's Government

This 19th day of October 1782

Top left: The Brandy Hole was just below the tunnel but was obliterated by the construction of the railway.

The Brandy Hole *(Part II of II)*

Immediately over this cavern, and adjoining the rude goat track that then encircled the Head, was a shaft sunk in a slanting direction into the earth, communicating with another subterraneous chamber - a sort of second storey to the lower one - but showing no trace of its existence on the surface, as the entrance was carefully concealed by a thick growth of brambles and bracken. This provided for the initiated a ready means of access from the land to the cavern, which was furnished where necessary with steps and platforms whereby a person above could, by means of a rope, assist those below to climb out on top, or if need be, drag up bales of goods for storage in the upper chamber.

In after years, when reports began to be whispered abroad as to the existence of this Ali Baba's cave, the locality became the scene of some fierce struggles between the Revenue men and the desperadoes engaged in the contraband traffic. It was a time when a Revenue officer's life was one of constant excitement; he needed to be a man of courage and determination, and the risks of his avocation were almost as great as those of a soldier's in the field.

Both the caves mentioned were utterly obliterated during the construction of the railway, but the name of "The Brandy Hole" still attaches to an inlet in the cliffs, and is the sole memorial of this great smugglers' rendezvous, the very tradition of which has been lost among the modern population.

With the advent of steam, telegraphs and police, smuggling has been shorn of much of the romance with which it once was associated; the picturesque figure of the bold smuggler with his slouched hat and feather, jack-boots and huge pistols, has disappeared from the stage of modern life and survives only in that of melodrama, and all the folk of today, whirled rapidly along the railway around Bray Head, or out for a summer evenings walk along the Cliff Walk, look down on his former haunts with scarcely a thought for the desperate scenes enacted there well over a hundred years ago.

BRAY - DID YOU KNOW...?

braydidyouknow@gmail.com

Billy Power and the silent movie era *(Part I of II)*

Long before the opening of the famous Ardmore Studios, Bray was already playing an important part in early film production. A local man, Billy Power, who had returned from Manchester, England with the intention of making moving films, was the leading figure in the venture. He planned to meet the demand existing for moving pictures. Billy ran a barber's shop on Novara Avenue, which was as much a film studio and laboratory as it was a barber's shop.

In 1917 he set up the Bray Musical and Dramatic Society for the purpose of using it as a recruiting ground for his films. In 1918 he wrote, produced and directed his first comedy film 'Willie Scouts While Jessie Pouts' and following the success of this venture he founded the Celtic Film Company and attempted a more ambitious two hour long movie 'Rosaleen Dhu.'

This movie told the tale of a Fenian who left Ireland to join the French Foreign Legion, with Kitty Scarf as the leading lady. The film was mostly shot in the Bray area, the beach at Arklow was used for desert scenes, a cottage on Bray Head for an eviction scene, and a coal boat in the harbour for the hero's farewell.

Rosaleen Dhu

The film was processed in wooden barrels at the rear of Power's Barber shop, some of the costumes for his productions were often borrowed from the Queens theatre, while others were made by members of the cast in their own homes.

To be continued...

Bray - Did You Know...?

braydidyouknow@gmail.com

Billy Power and the silent movie era *(Part II of II)*

Those early silent films were shot by a camera in a fixed position but Power invested in a camera capable of panning, for the sum of £88. The camera was operated by Matt Tobin, the blind organist at the church of the Most Holy Redeemer. Other members of the film company included Jim and Bob Tobin, Simon Dempsey, Lena O'Toole, Paddy Carr and Bill Quinn.

'Rosaleen Dhu' was premiered in McDermott's Cinema, which was housed in the Turkish

A photo of Billy Power's barber shop on Novara Avenue after his son 'Jazzer' took over the business.

Baths building (demolished 1979). Power was encouraged by the great reception the film received and planned his second feature 'An Irish Vendetta' with Power himself playing the villain.

Those involved in the production were to receive shares of the profit the movie would generate, but unfortunately tragedy struck. On June 6, 1920, during the filming of the story's climax at Leopardstown Racecourse, Power's horse bolted, throwing him onto the rails. Billy Power died two days later in the Mater Hospital, on the 8 June, 1920 and the film was never completed. Unbelievably, the last print of 'Rosaleen Dhu' was destroyed by the devastating floods at Little Bray in 1932.

Billy Power's Barber shop was then taken over and run by his son 'Jazzer' Power for many years, Jazzer's love for pigeons and all pet birds was obvious when one would enter his shop and be surrounded by all the bird cages on the walls.

The Picture House, Quinsboro' Rd., Bray. LESSEE J. E. MACDERMOTT. All the Latest Exclusive U-to-date Pictures. Matinees Wednesday and Saturday at 3.30. Pictures changed every Monday, Wednesday and Friday. POPULAR PRICES 1/-, 7d. 5d. and 4d.

© Bray – Did You Know 2012

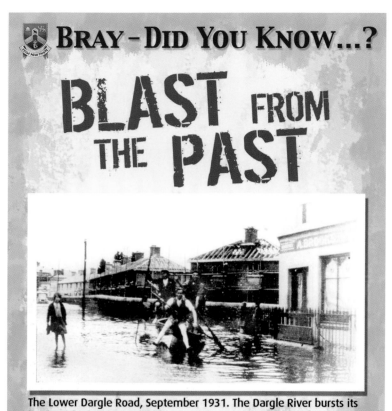

BRAY - DID YOU KNOW...?

BLAST FROM THE PAST

The Lower Dargle Road, September 1931. The Dargle River bursts its banks at high tide the night before. Over 500 people were forced to flee their homes. Of these, 300 were temporarily housed in the International Hotel which had been unoccupied since the war. Others were housed at Ravenswell Convent. Many Streets in the Dargle area were flooded, in some places to a depth of 5 or 6 feet. Note St. Brigid's Terrace under construction in the background of the photo.

braydidyouknow@gmail.com

BRAY
DID YOU KNOW?

© Bray - Did You Know 2012

Little Bray

Bray, on the Road to Glendalough, Co. Wicklow.

A char-a-banc on Upper Dargle Road c. 1925.

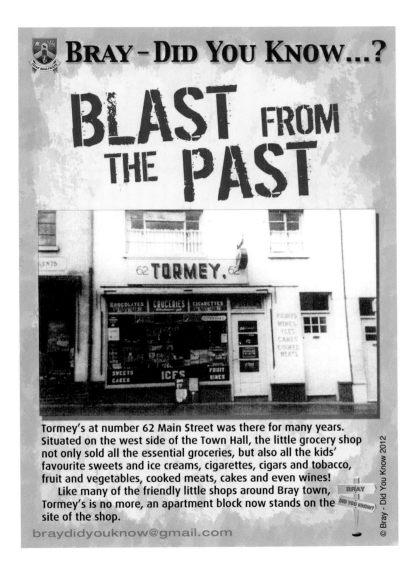

BLAST FROM THE PAST

62 TORMEY. 62

Tormey's at number 62 Main Street was there for many years. Situated on the west side of the Town Hall, the little grocery shop not only sold all the essential groceries, but also all the kids' favourite sweets and ice creams, cigarettes, cigars and tobacco, fruit and vegetables, cooked meats, cakes and even wines!

Like many of the friendly little shops around Bray town, Tormey's is no more, an apartment block now stands on the site of the shop.

braydidyouknow@gmail.com

© Bray - Did You Know 2012

213

Tormey's of Main Street

All the shops in this 1974 photo were demolished in c. 2007.

BRAY • NOW AND THEN

County Wicklow · Ireland

braydidyouknow@gmail.com

Two photos taken from the center of the Esplanade looking south towards Bray Head. The photograph below was taken in 1946 from the roof of the Ladies Baths. The recent photo was taken from the aquarium building.

There are a lot of changes over the years, a lot less traffic on the Strand Road, and some of the houses and hotels along the seafront have changed appearance or are simply gone, as is the hedging which divides the road with the Esplanade. Also note the children enjoying the Punch & Judy Show which is in full swing on the bottom right.

© Bray - Did You Know 2012

© Bray - Did You Know 2012

214

A tragedy off Bray Head (Part I of II)

The North Wicklow Coast is a treacherous one, full of sandbanks, submerged wrecks and other underwater hazards. Knowing one's precise position at sea is vitally important and whereas today this can be easily determined within seconds with great accuracy through the use of maritime navigation satellites, in former days this had to be calculated using several pieces of information.

A key requirement for any mariner has always been accurate coastal charts kept up to date through the use of additional information contained in regular notices known as *Admiralty Notices to Mariners* and a failure to do this was partly responsible for a maritime disaster off Bray in 1876, in the course of which one member of the Kingstown (Dun Laoghaire) lifeboat and three rescued seamen were lost, when the lifeboat capsized in heavy seas.

On Saturday September 30 1876, the brig 'Leona' under the command of Captain Thomas Richards with a cargo of timber for Liverpool from Nova Scotia was making its way up the North Wicklow coast. By his own admission later, Captain Richards was not familiar with the Irish coastline and had forgotten to mark on his navigation chart a lightship marking HMS Vanguard which had gone down eight miles east south east of the Kish light on September 1st 1875. Sometime prior to September 1876 this lightship, marking the wreck had been removed, possibly as an economy measure, but Capt. Richards thought that it was still in position there at that time. Coming up the coast along Greystones, Captain Richards took some bearings and misread the Kish light for the one that formerly marked the HMS Vanguard wreck and he plotted a course accordingly. This brought him into Bray off Bray Head and he proceeded to drop his anchors about 3/4 miles off shore believing that he was off Kingstown.

There was a strong gale blowing and he soon realised that he was not where he thought and worried that his vessel might become a total wreck and hoisted a distress signal, which was noticed at the Bray Coastguard station. The Chief Coastguard Officer sent telegrams to Kingstown and Greystones lifeboat stations - to effect a rescue. The Greystones lifeboat station consisted of the 'Sarah Tancred' a 33ft 10 oar boat. The Greystones crew turned out, but the weather conditions were so bad that it could not be launched and so the decision was taken to bring it on its carriage overland to Bray and this was done using four horses...

Top left: Captain Thomas Richards was in command of the 'Leona' and had forgotten to mark the wreck of the HMS Vanguard (top right) on his navigation chart; Above: A map showing the Kish Bank and two boat wrecks of the 'Vesper' (1876) and the 'Bolivar' in 1947.

BRAY - DID YOU KNOW...?

County Wicklow · Ireland

braydidyouknow@gmail.com

A tragedy off Bray Head (Part II of II)

However, on arrival in Bray along the sea front, weather conditions made it impossible for it to be launched. In Kingstown, which boasted one of the latest lifeboats in use at the time, the crew turned out and rowed out of the harbour, hoisted their sail and proceeded to sail to the casualty, which lay off Bray. They reached the 'Leona' at 3p.m. and drew alongside, Captain Richards and his crew boarded the lifeboat, with their personal belongings. At the time of casting off from the 'Leona' the lifeboat held nineteen persons and instead of heading inshore to Bray, Coxswain Henry Williams decided to return to Kingstown but after a short while decided, possibly in view of the heavy sea running, to land at Bray. As the lifeboat was turning about to do this, she was struck by some waves and capsized, throwing all those on board into the sea.

The Greystones lifeboat crew bringing the craft overland to Bray (Sketch: Ray O'Donnell).

Those on shore watching were horrified to see the lifeboat overturn, but there was little they could do until those on board floated inwards. As the survivors neared the beach some of those on land waded into the water and pulled them ashore and plied them with restoratives; as most likely they were suffering badly from exposure and hypothermia. All on board the lifeboat and 'Leona' had been wearing life jackets and this helped them to remain afloat in the water. At the upturned lifeboat, Captain Richards and three others held on until they could float ashore and be rescued. A roll call on Bray beach – the promenade had yet to be built – revealed that one member of the lifeboat crew and three from the 'Leona' were missing. The missing lifeboat man, Thomas White, was pulled from the rolling surf by a number of people but they were unable to revive him and his body was later moved to Kingstown.

The disaster created a big impact in Bray and a relief fund was set up. The incident was recalled later by one of the Town Commissioners in 1888 when some local fishermen were drowned off the Seafront. This led to a campaign resulting in the present day Harbour which was built in the 1890's. An

Above: A crew on their way to the sea for a practice run.

inquest was held on the body of Thomas White on 2 October. After hearing evidence from witnesses, the jury stated that Thomas White had drowned by the capsizing of the lifeboat. They also recommended that the wife and family of the deceased might be taken into consideration by the Lords of the Admiralty for his long service.

An R.N.L.I inquiry into the incident was critical of the decisions taken by Coxswain Williams and his handling of the lifeboat in such bad weather conditions and felt that he should have tried to land at Bray. The inquiry was also unhappy about the fact that luggage had been allowed onto the lifeboat.

Another lifeboat member, Bernard Mundone, died some months later of injuries received that day and his family received an ex gratia payment from the R.N.L.I. They also paid White's family a formal payment. The Greystones lifeboat station was closed in 1896 and today Bray Head marks the boundary between the Dun Laoghaire and Wicklow lifeboats, who continue to work closley together in rescues at sea.

BRAY - DID YOU KNOW...?

BLAST FROM THE PAST

A photo of the seafront before the Coastal Protection Scheme got under way in 1998, which was one of the most controversial schemes ever to be carried out on the east coast of Ireland. The idea was to protect the town's Victorian Promenade from the raging seas – but the plan bitterly divided the local community.

The scheme involved the importation and dumping of over 240,000 m³ of shingle onto the beach to a height level with the promenade. But will it protect the promenade? If so, it will have been at a price, as it has changed the look of our seafront forever.

braydidyouknow@gmail.com

© Bray - Did You Know 2012

BRAY
DID YOU KNOW?

The Promenade

Bray promenade in 1962 in all its glory.

the
Town Hall

The Bray Town Hall and market place was built by the 11th Earl of Meath's son, Reginald Brabazon in 1882-3. It was designed in the Tudor Revival style by Sir Thomas Newenham Deane and Son, but Brabazon also got personally involved in the design as evidence can be clearly seen by such items as the thirty stained-glass panels around the building, which display the coat of arms of all the Brabazon's Wives back as far as Norman times. The specially carved fireplace inside the chamber and the outside fountain, which is crowned by a wyvern from the Meath coat of arms.

BLAST FROM THE PAST

It's back to the early 1980s in these great snaps from the era that brought us the dreaded shoulder pads and mullet hair cuts! No mobile phones, flat screen tv's, PlayStation or X-box then. But, there was super music, great horror movies and the Cadbury's 'Wispa' bar!

The Town Hall (above) and the old air-raid siren to the left, which was used to call the firemen in Bray to duty; it could also be heard in parts of Shankill!
Tesco store (left) on the Vevay Road, note how old the cars look.

© Bray – Did You Know

braydidyouknow@gmail.com

The Town

Caprani's Pork Butchers just before they closed. The building is now demolished.

Royal Marine Terrace

A recent and a late 19th century photograph of the Royal Marine Terrace which overlooks the north end of the promenade. The Royal Marine Terrace, which was also called 'the red houses' in the late 19th and early 20th centuries (because they were all made of red brick) was named after *Breslin's Royal Marine Hotel* which was located just across the road on the site of the 'Katie Gallagher's' pub until it went on fire in 1916. Note the railings and seating on the old photo which was along most of the promenade is no longer at the northern end - due to the many stormy high seas over the years.

BLAST FROM THE PAST

THE VERANDA CAFE EAGLE'S NEST BRAY

The Eagle's Nest at Bray Head is now a private residence. But back in the 40s and 50s it was one of the top dance spots on the east coast. It began in 1932 when Johnny McGuirk built it as a ballroom and restaurant and it thrived for years. The chair-lift company Irish Holidays purchased it in 1946 and it became *The Veranda Café*. The ballroom eventually closed, as did the café when the chair-lifts last ran from the terminus at Raheen Pk in 1976.

braydidyouknow@gmail.com

© Bray - Did You Know 2012

BRAY
DID YOU KNOW?

The Eagle's Nest

The 'Bray Head Express' in 1942, which transported passengers from the seafront to the Eagle's Nest.

221

POSTCARDS FROM BRAY

The Scalp, Near Enniskerry   Co. Wicklow

The Scalp is a wild ravine on the road between Dublin and Enniskerry. Its very wild appearance, enormous masses of granite heaped up in grand and picturesque confusion on each side. Professor Hill has shown that the Scalp was once the channel of a great river that drained districts of land, now denuded of extensive rock deposits, and which discharged itself through the Irish Sea in distant ages.

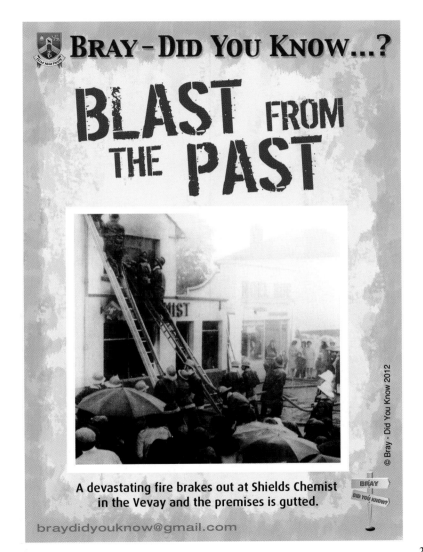

BLAST FROM THE PAST

A devastating fire brakes out at Shields Chemist in the Vevay and the premises is gutted.

© Bray - Did You Know 2012

BRAY
DID YOU KNOW?

braydidyouknow@gmail.com

The Vevay

Cullen's Butcher shop in the Vevay c. 1950s.

POSTCARDS FROM BRAY

Greetings FROM BRAY

I'SE LONELY WITHOUT YOU.

BRAY HEAD & ESPLANADE.

BRAY - DID YOU KNOW...?

BLAST FROM THE PAST

The making of 'My Left Foot' at St. Kevin's Square - just off the Main Street - in 1989, which starred Daniel Day-Lewis, Brenda Fricker and Alison Whelan.

Other film locations in Bray included Killruddery House, and of course, the famous Ardmore Studios.

braydidyouknow@gmail.com

St. Kevin's Square

Daniel Day-Lewis who played Christy Brown in *My Left Foot*.

BRAY - DID YOU KNOW...?

County Wicklow · Ireland

braydidyouknow@gmail.com

POSTCARDS FROM BRAY

AN IRISH FLAG FROM BRAY

ERIN GO BRAGH

under the dear old Irish Flag
Are beauties, rich and rare,
For Nature's hand endowed this land
With charms beyond compare.

POST CARD.

"NATIONAL" SERIES.

CORRESPONDENCE.   ADDRESS.

2176

Having a fun time in Bray
weather is very nice and people
are so friendly.
On our way for a swim at the
cove at Bray head
will take some snaps to show
you all - bye for now and see
you soon!

Mᵣˢ W. Davis

Palmer Green

London

The Beach

SEAFRONT AT BRAY, CO. WICKLOW, IRELAND.

A Dollard postcard of Bray's esplanade and beach c. 1960.

Calendar of Events

1850 - 1920

The following Calendar of Events covers most of the period in this book.
To see the complete Calendar of Events please visit our facebook page at
www.facebook.com / braydidyouknow

1850

- Allen's Menswear is established on Bray Main Street – and is at number 100 Main Street today.
- The church in the Main Street is extended in granite with 33ft added to the nave's length and a tower is erected. The houses in front of the church on the Main Street are purchased and demolished.

10 August
- The Loreto Sisters purchase (approx. £8,000) San Souci (once home of the Putland family) for a private boarding school and convent.

Loreto Convent on the Vevay Road was purchased for £8,000

1851

- There are 668 dwellings in the town.

7 January   · Loreto Convent opens.
15 March   · William Brabazon becomes the 11th Earl of Meath when his father John Chambre Brabazon dies.
September   · The vessel Fame is shipwrecked off the Wicklow coast.
December   · The vessel Pilgrim is shipwrecked off the Wicklow coast.

1852

- Railway company begins work on rail bridge and wooden footbridge over the mouth of the Bray river.

October
- John Quin (jr) inherits his father's hotel (Quin's) and all of his extensive landholdings to the east of the Main Street. He also begins transforming his pathway leading from the rear of his hotel to the sea as a public road.

Andrew Nicholl's View of Main Street from the East which shows Quin's Walk. Note the cows grazing on the site of Florence Road. c. 1840.

10 November   · At 4.10 am Ireland experiences an earthquake.
1 December
- Mr John Quin (Snr) dies at the age of 91. He was the owner of Quin's Hotel opposite the courthouse.

1853

- The new rail and footbridge over the Bray River (Dargle) is completed. However, the bridge now blocks the entrance to the Old Dock and Seymour's Dock which was up river on the south river bank.
- Construction on the railway station at Bray begins.

11 October   · The Dublin, Wicklow and Bray railway lines are joined.

1854

- The Quinsborough Road is opened – originally called the 'Forty-Foot Road' – it was to become the main artery between the old Bray and the new.
- At a cost of £2,000, work starts on the addition to the nave and tower at the Holy Redeemer Church on Bray Main Street.

10 July
- The first train leaves Bray during the official opening of the Dublin to Bray railway.

October
- Sites for villas being sold near Bray Head - advertised as being within two minutes' walk from the station.

1855

- The Antler Hotel on Bray seafront is built.

January
- Another major cholera epidemic breaks out in the town.

30 May
- Breslin's Bray Hotel (later to be renamed Breslin's Royal Marine Hotel) is opened by Edward Breslin on a spot just east of the railway station.

May
- Brighton Terrace is laid out – by 1937 it will become part of Parnell Road.

25 October
- The railway line around Bray Head is complete and the line to Wicklow is opened by the Lord Lieutenant who will travel from Harcourt Street to Wicklow on the line.

Breslin's Royal Marine Hotel was originally only the left part of the building above - the extension to the right was built on later.

1856

- The Wicklow Arms Inn at Delgany is established.

31 May
- The 12.30 express train from Dublin - Wicklow, turning first curve of Bray Head, surprises a group of little children between two and five years old playing on the railway track - at a distance of not more than 40 yds. The driver Joseph Browne, with risk to his own life, jumps off the engine and snatches, from the jaws of death, one of the children. No human exertion on the part of the driver and guard could have stopped the train in time and it was entirely due to the cool intrepidity of the driver that the child's life was saved.

11 September
- The new Bray Bridge, built by David Edge, is officially opened by Mrs. Mason of the Anchor Tavern, Bray & Mrs. Butler of Loughlinstown.

1857

- Property Agents H.J. Byrne & Company is established in Bray.

		• 22 public lamps are erected in Bray: 17 on Main Street, 2 on Quinsborough Road and 2 on Seymour Road.
11	March	• The first train to Wicklow is delayed as stone falls on the railway line at Bray Head. The Engine is derailed and slightly damaged. This incident results in the line being shifted 8 ft - 10 ft inland.
9	November	• The Bray Town Commissioners (B.T.C.'s) are established – the 11th Earl of Meath is first chairman.

1858

		• Bray's 19th century Boom Period begins.
		• The Hon. Sidney Herbert beings construction of the 'New Road to the Dargle'. The new Herbert Road plan will cost £2,000. Several houses in Bray Main Street will be demolished in order to build the direct line from the seashore (via Quinsborough Road) to the Dargle.
23	February	• Completion of Admiralty, or Compensatory Dock east of the railway bridge at river mouth. The rail company was ordered by the Admiralty to build a dock for the traders of Bray and merchant shipping after access to Seymour's Dock was blocked by the new railway bridge in 1852/1853.
11	August	• 24-year-old Charles Barrington (right) from Fassaroe, Bray is the first man to reach the summit of the Eiger.
12	September	• St Andrew's Presbyterian Church on the Quinsborough Road is built and open for worship.

An 1870 map showing the three docks at the Bray River and what is now the Harbour area.

Charles Barrington 1834 - 1901
First man to climb the Eiger Peak

1859

		• Brennan's Terrace – a row of twelve large houses – is built on the esplanade by James Brennan. While William Dargan builds the elegant 'Dargan Terrace' on the Quinsborough Road. Also work on a terrace of fine houses begins on a piece of ground known as Kelly's Rampart. The terrace will be called Martello Terrace.
24	February	• Bray Commons Enclosure Act: A public meeting is held in the Bray Court House (beside the Royal Hotel) for the purpose of taking into consideration a bill now before parliament, for enclosing the Commons of the Dargle and converting it into a public park.

| 27 | October | • William Dargan completes work on south end of the esplanade, including £400 of his own money spent on fencing esplanade with chains and granite posts. |
| 2 | November | • The Imperial Roman & Turkish Baths (beside Duncairn Terrace) on the Quinsborough Road are opened to the public. |

1860

The Turkish Baths at Quinsborough Road - photo c. 1950.

• Gas is piped to the town from the gas works at Bray docks.
• Swimming Baths are erected at the northern end of the strand.
• Vance & Wilson's chemist is established at Main Street in Bray.
• Private avenue of Novara House (previously Bayview) opens between the town and the sea.
• The Compensatory / Admiralty Dock becomes 'unusable' as it had fallen into disrepair as no maintenance arrangements were put in place.

| | August | • The Bray Head Hotel is opened by John Lacy. |

1861

• The construction of Fitzwilliam Terrace on the Strand Road, and Prince of Wales Terrace on Quinsborough Road begins.
• A terrace of 19 houses is built by William Dargan adjacent to the Admiralty Dock and is named Dock Terrace.
• Ravenswell Road is laid out, as is the single-arch bridge constructed at the northern end of the bridge, linking Castle Street to Ravenswell Road.

18	February	• The first stone of Mr James Brennan's new International Hotel on Quinsborough Road is erected. But he passes away a few months after its opening in May 1862.
3	May	• Traces of gold found in Bray river (Dargle) when construction of the 1,825 ft wall from Bray bridge to the railway (cost £3,000) begins.
14	May	• William Dargan presents the esplanade to the town.

Bray seafront as it was when Dargan took it over to complete the original esplanade - c. 1860.

1862

- Charles Putland opens a new road to help with famine relief on his demesne running from Newcourt-Vevay to the seafront called 'The Road of Ten Houses after the houses which were built at Putland Villas. it is later named Putland Road after the Putland family. The houses at Sydenham Villas are also completed.
- A preparatory school for Protestant boys is opened at 'Fort View' on Sidmonton Road by Thomas Reginald Courtney - this school would later become Aravon School.
- Marine Terrace is built on the Strand Road between Albert Avenue and Quinsborough Road. The western side of Galtrim Road is laid out to join 'Novarre' (Novara Avenue).

31 May
- The official opening of the magnificent £24,000 International Hotel, which coincides with the inauguration of the International Exhibition at London.

The International Hotel which opened on Quinsborough Road on 31 May, 1862.

1863

- Alexandra Terrace on Novara Road is built.
- The Methodist Church on the Eglinton Road is built by E.F. Tarleton, but is erected chiefly though the instrumentality of the Rev. Samuel Dunlop.
- Construction of Goldsmith Terrace – originally a uniform row of twelve houses – on the Quinsborough Road is completed.
- Dr. William Wilde (father of Oscar) builds the Esplanade Terrace on the esplanade. Dr. William, eye and ear surgeon and antiquarian, is one of the early developers of the town and a member of the B.T.C.'s. He also built "Elsinore" c. 1872 - which is now the Strand Hotel – as an investment.
- Bray's Boom Period is waning.
- Milton Terrace on Seapoint Road is built.

Sir William Wilde was one of the early developers in Bray.

1864

- The Elrington Road (later Eglinton Road) is completed.

	July	• St. Andrew's Methodist Church on the Eglinton Road is opened.
1	August	• The French School at Sidmonton Place in Bray is founded by Madame Héloise de Mailly.
29	October	• No. 3 Martello tower at Bray north beach has been found shaken from the foundation, having been sapped by the seas running in along the coast during the recent gales. It is considered to be in an unsafe state.

1865

• Bray's first gas lamps are installed. But charges were considered very high, and the quality was often far from satisfactory and there were many complaints from both domestic consumers and the B.T.C.'s.

• £30 is allowed by the Bray Commons Commissioners for 'providing a platform to reach pure water in the centre of Bray River beneath the bridge', from which it was drawn by 'carts and barrels'. Three access points to the river for watering animals are also provided.

| 27 | March | • Collision at Bray between Enniscorthy train and ore train. A Mrs. Toome of Wicklow slightly injured. |
| 8 | December | • The Martello Tower No. 3 on the north beach at Bray collapses into the sea during a storm. |

1866

Aravon School on the Meath Road – just as it was before being demolished.

• Adelaide Road is constructed and incorporated into the already constructed Meath Road. It is renamed Adelaide Road after John Brennan's daughter in 1907.

• Plans to construct the 'New Bridge Road' from the new bridge through the commons to go ahead - it would later become the 'Lower Dargle Road'.

• Thomas Reginald Courtney moves his school to 'Aravon' on the Meath Road - it becomes known as Aravon School - Aravon is obviously a reversal of 'Novara' as it stood on land formerly belonging to Novara House.

| 28 | May | • Public meeting is held at the Turkish Baths to consider subject of utilizing buildings for public purposes by formation of assembly rooms, concert, exhibition and literature halls with reading, refreshment rooms, and other accommodation. |

1867

• Turkish Baths are converted into Assembly Rooms for concerts and other entertainments as they become unpopular.

- The Commons and the Dargle area of Little Bray are flooded when the river breaks it's banks.
- Bray is struck by another outbreak of cholera.

7 February
- William Dargan dies at the age of 68 in his town house at 2 Fitzwilliam Square, Dublin.

9 August
- Major railway accident at Bray Head; the engine, tender and three carriages of the Enniscorthy-Dublin train left the track as it ran onto No. 2 viaduct, south of Brabazon tunnel and fell 33ft from the bridge. Fireman Mr Murphy was killed at the scene and two other passengers, James Donnelly and a Mrs hackman, died later from their injuries.

The scene of the 1867 railway accident south of the Brabazon tunnel.

1868
- Six years since the International Hotel on the Quinsborough Road opened and it has changed hands three times.
- The Prince and Princess of Wales visit Killruddery.
- The Vartry Water Scheme is completed at Roundwood.
- Wooden footbridge at the railway station in Bray is replaced with a steel bridge.

17 February
- A passenger train collides with some ballast freight wagons at Bray Station.

1869
- The Protestant church on Main Street is completely refurbished and is dedicated to St Paul.
- Around 20,000 people, mainly outsiders, demonstate in Purcell's field (now Connolly and St. Kevin's Square) in favour of the release of political prisoners; the effigy of Judge William Kehoe was burnt here in 1872.
- Hackney Cars and Carriages Regulations (bye laws) for Bray and 4 mile radius.
- Fr. James Healy is appointed to St Peter's Church in Little Bray and it becomes a parish.
- John Quin, hotelier and businessman passes away.

1870
- An outbreak of cholera at Bray. Dr Christopher Thompson of Duncairn Terrace treats many of the victims.
- The B.T.C.'s lose their case in court for the banning of boats from the esplanade because of 'the prescriptive right of the fishermen to have them there'.

	January	• The first fair is held in the Fair Green on the Dargle Road.
	June	• Water flows from the new Vartry Reservoir in Roundwood to Bray for the first time.
	November	• The Boghall Brick Company is established at Brickfield, Killarney Road in Bray.

1871

• County Wicklow magistrate Edward Lysaght Griffin of Violet Hill, Bray, submits a formal complaint to the Board of Trade about the problems and delays for vehicular traffic at the Bray Railway Gates. By this time at least eighteen trains a day are arriving/departing from Bray. The Board of Trade indicated that, in the absence of up to date signaling equipment at Bray, an underpass should be constructed to replace the level crossing gates. The DW & WR proposed to replace the existing level crossing with a short underpass or vehicular tunnel some twenty-seven feet wide, fourteen feet in height extending in a downwards direction from a point opposite the front door of the former International Hotel. This however, never materialized, had it come to pass, would have provided the town with a unique feature.

| | September | • Roger Casement's first day of school at Aravon School on Meath Road, Bray. |

1872

An early photograph of Bray Railway Station taken from the International Hotel.

• Storms and flooding badly damage the gasworks at the dock area – the town is without lighting for several days and forced to fall back on paraffin lighting.
• Lord Meath requests the extension of the town to Killruddery, but the request is opposed on financial grounds by existing ratepayers and is rejected.

| 27 | January | • The final edition of the Bray Gazette newspaper is published. |
| 16 | September | • The boiler exploded on Locomotive No. 4 at Bray Railway Station. |

1873

• Bray seafront is flooded and the Bray River (Dargle River) breaks its banks during a violent storm.

| 27 | January | • An Italian Barque (sailing ship) named 'Pimorrero' is stranded on the Dublin side of Bray Head. But the crew are rescued and taken by a tug to Kingstown (Dun Laoghaire). |

1 March	• Newspaper report in the 'The Kingston and Bray Gazette': house property along the coast extending between Kingstown and Bray, and including those important townships, is becoming valuable and difficult to attain. A house fronting the sea is almost unattainable.
17 May	• The yacht 'Nicomi' from Dalkey got into trouble off Bray Head, so the Greystones lifeboat was called out and rescued the four people on board.

1874

• St Peter's National School (now the Parish Hall) beside St Peter's Church is rebuilt and opened.
• The Cripple's Home on the Lower Dargle Road is founded by Lucinda Sullivan for destitute crippled children. It was the first and only one of its kind in Ireland.

2 October	• Charles Putland (Jnr) of Bray Head House dies.
5 October	• The B.T.C.'s establish a public health committee: the Urban Sanitary Authority. The authority will concentrate on housing nuisances, also inter alia, looking at complaints regarding schools, the assembly hall, car stands, etc.

The Cripple's Home on the Lower Dargle Road during the devestating floods of 1905.

1875

• The Bray Improvement Committee is formed – consisting of prominent residents and businessmen.
• Fore shore and Esplanade Bye Laws passed. They control preaching, collecting money, riding bicycles and tricycles and roulette tables.
• The International Hotel is sold again.
• Matthew O'Reilly Dease, owner of the lands at Ravenswell, passes away. Ravenswell is put up for sale and it is purchased by the Earl of Meath for his son and heir, Lord Brabazon, who had spent most of his life abroad.

1 September	• A 6,000 ton battleship called the 'H.M.S. Vanguard' sinks as a result of an accidental ramming with 'The Iron Duke' in thick fog, 8 miles due east of Bray Head – near the Kish Bank – no loss of life.

1876

• A major outbreak of cholera in Bray – originates in the Boghall area – over 200 people die of the disease.

- A skating rink is erected on the strand and is reputedly 'one of the best in these islands'.
- Dr. William Wilde, who built the Esplanade Terrace dies, leaving his Bray property to his son Oscar.
- The 300 yard long tunnel at Bray Head, known as the Brabazon Tunnel is bypassed by two short tunnels.
- The building of the new Coastguard Station begins just south of the railway bridge on the Putland Road.

30 September · The brigantine 'Leona', with timber from St. John's, is wrecked in broad daylight off the north beach at Bray.

16 December · After a major outbreak of cholera in Bray, Dr. Christopher Thompson dies after contracting the disease himself while treating the sick in Bray. A memorial is later erected in his memory opposite the Royal Hotel.

1877

- The new coastguard station opens near the Putland Road.
- The Turkish Baths is described in a newspaper as 'a perfect eyesore' and later as a 'speckled elephant' (as opposed to a white one).

January · Massive storms flood the entire seafront area; fishing boats and cabins washed away, as was parts of the railway line at Bray Head. The Gas Works at the dock area are almost demolished, the site is abandoned to the sea and is now within the harbour area. A new site will be found near the old Seymour Dock site behind the railway at the harbour.

1878

- Lord Brabazon erects gates across Ravenswell Road, claiming it is not a right of way. The road is the only access from Little Bray to the shore north of the river mouth. The B.T.C.'s write to him referring to memorials of protest from the residents against the closing of the right of way. Desultory correspondence goes on for over a year, but the road is eventually opened back to the public.

April · The Bray Pavilion Company is formed, its prospectus noting the 'deficiency in provision for amusement and recreation of visitors to Bray' and work commences on the new Ladies' Baths midway along the esplanade on a site now occupied by the National Sealife Aquarium.

- The Martello Tower no. 1 is considered dangerous. The foundations are being undermined by the sea and a long crack is found up the side of the tower.

The Ladies' Baths was situated on the centre of the promenade. Photo c. 1890

1879

- Reginald Brabazon writes to the B.T.C.'s offering to erect a covered market house – as Bray had not had a market house since the demolition forty years earlier of one near Bray Bridge – and lease it to the Commissioners.
- Because of rock fall and erosion part of the railway line at Bray Head is diverted again.
- Bray Town Hall will be designed by Thomas Newenham Deane & Son.

Bray's Town Hall c. 1905 which stands on the south end of Bray's Main Street.

1880

- Report shows that 15,000 tons of coal was imported and landed at Bray and 20,000 tons of limestone passes through the port annually.

22 January
- B.T.C.'s to request parliament to implement the Act to improve the harbour and offer financial assistance.

1 March
- At a meeting of the B.T.C.'s Charles Dufrense of the International Hotel puts forward plan of a concrete sea wall to protect the strand against the encroachments of the sea. P.F. Comber draws up plans for an 18ft high sea wall at 1,043 yards long.

14 October
- The Bray Boys National School at the rear of the Holy Redeemer Church (the present Little Flower Hall) is opened at a cost of £1,200. There were 21 pupils in the school's 1st Class.

1881

- Authorization for the building of the sea wall and promenade is passed by Parliament. Under the 1881 Township Act the B.T.C.'s or its successor B.U.D.C. (Bray Urban District Council) have the right to levy a toll for maintenance of the sea wall - as yet they have never enforced this right.
- The Bray Township Bill 1881 comes into force. The bill gives powers to compulsorily acquire and clear dwellings.
- The People's Park on the Commons is presented to the town by the 11th Earl of Meath.
- Construction begins on the new Town Hall and Market Place (above) at the top of Bray's Main Street - the Earl of Meath laying the foundation stone.

The People's Park on the Lower Dargle Road was presented to the town by Lord Meath.

- At a total cost of £1.154, the eight bells of Christ Church are hung and rang for the first time. The whole weight of the bells slightly exceed 5.5 tons.

1882

- Lord Brabazon has a park-keepers lodge constructed at the east end of the People's Park in return for an extra £10 per annum rent on the Town Hall / Market House at the top of the Main Street, this manoeuvre effectively being a loan of the necessary funds. It was designed by Thomas Newenham Deane and Son, who designed the Town Hall.
- The Commons and the Little Bray area at the Dargle are flooded again.

25 April
- Patrick Mulligan (married), John Carthy (married), John Boden (40) and Michael Carthy put to sea in a small boat from Bray. They never returned.

1883

- The Bray Improvement Committee (formed 1875) is renamed 'Bray Amusements Committee'.
- Killisk House on Meath Road is built.
- Duncairn Avenue is laid out but was unnamed on the 1885 O.S. maps.

1884

- Work on the new sea wall and Grand Marine Promenade begins. Plans include erection of an 18ft high and 18ft wide promenade from the harbour to the ladies baths, at a cost of some £20,000. The 441 yard plan includes a long impressive walkway, edged with ornamental iron railings and furnished with fixed seating overlooking the beach – it will take two years to construct.
- Construction on the new Town Hall and Market Place at the top of Bray Town is completed. But costs spiraled from the original £2,720 tendered in 1879 to a final total of £6,359.
- The demolition of no. 1 Martello Tower at the Cockbrook - it was on a site near the end of the Promenade railings opposite where the Esplanade Hotel is now.
- Bray Brewery based at the Mill near Bray Bridge closes down.

15 December
- The market place at the new Town Hall opens for business.

The No. 1 Martello Tower can be clearly seen in this old photo c. 1880. It was knocked down in 1884.

1885

- Electric lighting is installed on the esplanade.
- The graveyard at Old Connaught Church is reported full and becomes subject to overcrowding.

August
- First section of sea wall and esplanade is completed (441 yds). McAlpines win tender for the second section (602 yds).

September
- Official opening ceremony of sea wall and promenade by Lord Lieutenant, Lord Carnarvon. Bray is the first town in Ireland to erect a marine promenade to cater for invalids.

December
- Two boats, with crews of five each, filled and sank whilst trying to land at Bray beach; but fortunately about twenty fishermen were waiting for them with lines and other appliances, and all were saved.

1886

- Construction of Florence Road begins - it is extended across the Quin estate as far as Eglinton Road, realigned slightly to bypass the Methodist church (1863). But six years elapse before the B.T.C.'s purchase the necessary properties (for demolition) at the Main Street end to finish the scheme. It is not until 1902 that it joined the Main Street.
- Bray Emmets GAA Club is founded.

Bray Emmets S.F.C. Winners in Dublin 1901

August
- Second section (602 yds) of sea-wall and promenade completed and opened.

15 August
- The Sisters of Charity arrive at 'Rack Rent House' on the Dublin Road.

1887

- After a winter of heavy storms a number of cracks appear in the first and second sections of the promenade. Major flooding occurs on the Seafront, the Commons and the Little Bray area at the Dargle.
- An obelisk is erected on a small summit near Bray Head by committee chairman W.P. Morris, a Justice of the Peace, to commemorate the Jubilee of Queen Victoria in 1887.

May
- The Joyce family – with son James – move into no. 1 Martello Terrace, Bray.

20 August
- Building work begins on St Andrew's School: The foundation stone of St Andrew's School on Eglinton Road is laid by the Earl of Meath.

1888

- A further application made to Parliament for an act to construct a harbour - the B.T.C's. would borrow the necessary finance themselves.

	January	• The railway line at Bray Head is diverted again because of rock fall and erosion.
		• St. Paul's Church of Ireland graveyard is declared closed due to it being old, urban and overcrowded.
		• St Andrew's School on Eglinton Road is opened.
26	June	• At a concert in Bray Boat House, James Joyce is a member of the cast.

1889

• The B.T.C.'s turn down a proposal for privately run tennis courts on the esplanade.

• The Great West Window of Christ Church on Church Road, Bray is completed.

2 September • Ardee Street, built on the Commons by the Dublin Artisans Dwelling Company is completed.

1890

• Bill passed in the House of Commons for the building of a harbour at Bray.

• Provision is made for the extension of the sea wall further south towards Bray Head.

• The 'Housing of the Working Classes Act' comes in; This Act will provide powers inter alia for dealing with unhealthy areas, unhealthy houses and house-building programmes in the town.

November • Hibernian Bank agree to grant a £30,000 loan to the B.T.C.'s for harbour scheme.

1891

• Work commences on the Bray – Enniskerry Light Railway line, including an embankment of 200 yds along the Bray River, but the scheme is bitterly opposed by the B.T.C.'s and Wicklow County Council and they direct workmen to tear up the tracks.

23 April • B.T.C.'s enter into a contract with Messrs William James Doherty, Civil Engineers, for the construction of a harbour at the mouth of Bray River of about seven acres.

3 August • With parliamentary approval, work on the Bray harbour commences.

10 October • The rules for Cycle Polo are devised by Bray man Richard Mecredy and a pioneer game is held at The Scalp (between Kilternan and Bray).

December • The Joyce family move from Martello Terrace, Bray to Carysfort Avenue, Blackrock, Co. Dublin.

Cycle Polo game on the Bray Promenade in 1908

1892

- The Meath Industrial School for Girls on the Vevay Road was founded by William, Earl of Meath. The School would later become St Patrick's Primary School.
- The B.T.C.'s erect a pair of shelters on Bray Seafront/Esplanade; one opposite the Marine Terrace at the north end and another just south of the bandstand.
- The former corn mill and brewery – near the bridge on the Dargle – is converted into the Bray Electric Works to supply the town with electricity from a turbine on the river. The company will be 'Bray Electric Light Company'.
- The lamps on the Esplanade (which by now were replaced) are converted to electricity.

15 April
- Henry John Cochrane of Woodbrook dies.

The Meath Industrial School on Vevay Road c. 1900.

1893

- Workmen at Lord Plunket's estate discover a moat inside the grounds opposite the entrance to 'Woodbrook'. Five skeletons were found in the moat along with bones of cattle, deer, goats and pigs split open for the marrow, which would suggest a great funeral feast. Other items found included shells for necklaces, bronze food containers and, most interesting of all, two small stone slabs with markings that unfortunately proved impossible to decipher.

15 May
- Bray promenade and town is lit by electric light.

1894

The 1927 Signal Cabin which still stands adjacent to the Quinsborough Road today.

- Gordon and Company of London, the owners of the Bray Electric Light Company, approach the B.T.C.'s to buy them out, thereby municipalising the service by becoming suppliers of electricity to the town. The B.T.C.'s dragged their heels, but with parliamentary approval, were forced by circumstances to buy the company from the liquidator. New machinery was installed and a new power station chimney constructed – it still stands today.
- Little Bray parish is reunited with 'Big' Bray parish.
- New signal cabin is built at Bray Railway Station.
- 'The Bray School' on Meath Road is renamed Aravon School ('Novara' spelt backwards, the buildings being on lands formerly attached to Novara House).

1 January   • Rev. N. Donnelly is appointed Parish Priest of Bray, Little Bray and Greystones.

1895

- A second extension is added to St Andrew's Church on the Quinsborough Road.
- The Esplanade / Lacy's Hotel is built on the site of the old Coastguard station – which closed in 1876 – next to the Strand Hotel.
- Introduction of the Housing of the Working Class Act.
- The footbridge – owned by the Brabazon family – over the railway at Bray Head is removed.

Pictured only a few years after it was built - the Esplanade Hotel still stands on the Bray Seafront.

1896

- Bray Township Electric Lighting Order, 1896: The B.T.C.'s take over ownership of the Bray Electric Works at the old mill; the scheme costing the township £20.000.
- Bray Sailing Club is founded.
- The Church of the Most Holy Redeemer on Bray's Main Street is further enlarged and decorated to cope with the growing numbers attending the church.
- Another proposal for a promenade pier in Bray. This proposal, the most serious, is for a combined tramway system, which would also run through the town of Bray, and a promenade pier. But the whole plan was soon dropped as was the initial enthusiasm that was shown for the project.
- The Cliff Walk from Bray to Greystones opens – originally named the 'Railway Walk' it is 7km long.

1897

- Bray Golf Club is founded at Ravenswell Road.
- The Bray Head Hotel goes bankrupt and is sold by the courts.

7 June   • Edward Breslin (1818 - 1897) dies at the age of 79.

10 August   • The harbour at Bray is completed and opened. An additional £22,000 had to be borrowed to complete the project - original estimate was £24,929.

1 October   • The lighthouse at the end of the south pier at Bray Harbour comes into use. The light, with a radius of 5 miles, gives 30 flashes per minute, each lasting 1.5 seconds.

1898

- Work on the Holy Redeemer Church is completed at a cost of £20,000.
27 December
- Tragedy at Bray Railway Station when inspector Bernard Lynch is accidentally killed.

1899

- The Urban District Council is established (replacing the B.T.C.'s) under the Local Government Act of 1898, and J.E. McCormick becomes first chairman.
- Hackney Cars plying from Bray, Co. Wicklow.
20 December
- The establishment of the Bray Technical Instruction Committee.

1900

- The Housing of the Working Class Act (1895) sees new streets containing about a hundred dwellings erected on the Commons. They are Dargan Street, Maitland Street and Ardee Street.
- Because of the growing popularity of bathing at Naylor's Cove, a railway platform is constructed above the cove – under the rail bridge.
- Final edition of the Wicklow Star Newspaper.
14 February
- A train from Bray to Harcourt Street, containing 30 wagonloads of cattle pushed the train relentlessly downhill from Ranelagh. It runs the buffers at Harcourt Street Station and crashes through the wall.
July
- A provisional order is confirmed authorizing slum clearance areas in Little Bray, purchase of land (including houses) for local authority housing and for opening up of roads.

1901

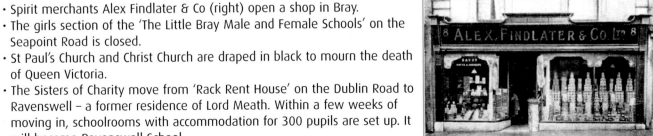

- Spirit merchants Alex Findlater & Co (right) open a shop in Bray.
- The girls section of the 'The Little Bray Male and Female Schools' on the Seapoint Road is closed.
22 January
- St Paul's Church and Christ Church are draped in black to mourn the death of Queen Victoria.
April
- The Sisters of Charity move from 'Rack Rent House' on the Dublin Road to Ravenswell – a former residence of Lord Meath. Within a few weeks of moving in, schoolrooms with accommodation for 300 pupils are set up. It will become Ravenswell School.

1902

1 May
- The Bray Technical School is founded when a lease is taken on the Infants' School at Brighton Terrace.

3 May
- The west end of the Florence Road scheme to the Main Street is opened. A further slight deviation to the northwest had to be made so that the junction with Main Street lay opposite to the Holy Redeemer Church.

6 October
- The King Edward Road, joining Killarney Road to Herbert Road is opened.

November
- J.S. Wolfe opens the Bray Cycle Factory opposite the Bridge School in Castle Street.

3 December
- An extension is added to The Meath protestant Industrial School on the Vevay Road, there are 91 names on the roll books.

The King Edward Road, with Christ Church in the background, shortly after it opened.

1903

- Construction on St Paul's School on the Herbert Road begins.
- The paths on the esplanade are concreted for the first time.

April
- The Bray Harbour Committee hires the Wicklow Harbour Commissioners dredger for one week at a cost of £20.

1904

- Bray is linked to electric light when a generator was erected, powered by water from the river.
- Wyndham Park is constructed as part of a uniform row of 13 properties.
- The first motor vehicle to be licensed by Wicklow County Council was to Michael J. Rahillly of Wilford Cottage, Bray.
- A new Post Office is built on the Quinsborough Road.
- Construction on St Paul's National School on the Herbert Road (now part of the car park at the rear of the Holy Redeemer Church) is completed.

11 September
- Sir Henry Cochrane dies.

1905

- B.U.D.C. refuses an address to King Edward to commemorate his coronation on account of the Oath.
- Dargle and Bray Laundry opens up on the Dargle Road (now Riverdale Apartments).
- The cemetery at the rere of St Peter's Church is reported full. Adjoining land to the west of the Church is purchased for a new cemetery.

- The Dargan Street housing scheme is completed.

25 August
- A disastrous flood hits Little Bray after the Dargle River bursts its banks. Water rises between 6 and 11ft higher than normal (when the flow was reinforced by the bursting of the 33 inch Vartry Water Main as the bridge which carried it across the Dargle was swept away). Approx 2,000 are rendered homeless. One man, James Plunkett, lost his life – his body was found on the golf links the next day.

After the 1905 flooding at Sheridan's Lane, Little Bray.

1906

- A special single platform, or halting site is opened by the Dublin & South Eastern Railway. It is located on the down side of the line, behind Naylor's Cove – adjacent to the road overbridge that gives access to Bray Head.
- The eastern end of Galtrim Road is constructed and realigned to meet western end at Novara Avenue.
- The Bray Amusements Committee abandon plans for a promenade pier.

20 March
- During a storm, the Schooner 'Velenheli' carrying coal for John Plunkett of Quinsborough Road, runs aground near Bray Harbour, just a few yards South of Martello Terrace.

1907

- Sir Stanley Cochrane - of the Cantrell and Cochrane mineral water fame - establishes a first-class cricket ground at his home at Woodbrook, complete with an elegant pavilion overlooking it, known as Woodbrook Club and Ground.
- The first sod of the new Purcell's Field housing scheme (Connolly Sq. & St. Kevin's Sq.) was turned.
- Mr. Moore's Bray Bridge School – located on the north side of Bray Bridge – closes. The pupils are transferred to the new St. Paul's Parochial School on Herbert Road.
- Mr. McDonnell – the Town Clerk – purchases three bandstands from the Dublin Exhibition for the Seafront. One is placed opposite the railway crossing (at Quinsborough Road junction) known as the 'Day Bandstand', another is placed in the centre of the esplanade (right), which still stands, called the 'Afternoon Bandstand' and the third opposite the Esplanade Hotel and was reserved for visiting variety shows and was called the 'Evening Bandstand'.

1908

- The formal opening of the new bandstands on the Promenade, on which the 11th Hussars, Scotch and Lancashire Fusiliers Band and several Dublin vocalists performed to over 4,000 people.
- A meeting on Coast Erosion is held at Bray Court House by the Royal Commission.

1909

- Principal alterations are made to join Galtrim Road with Adelaide Road and the opening of Kingsmill Road into the extension.
- Construction on the new James Connolly Square and St. Kevin's Square at Purcell's Field off Bray's Main Street ends.

17   September
- The Australian Cricket Team plays a Sir Stanley Cochrane XI at Sir Stanley's cricket grounds at Woodbrook, Bray.

1910

- The Bethall family, who own the International Hotel on Quinsborough Road and the Bray Head Hotel at the southern end of the promenade, purchase the Royal Marine Hotel and it is renamed the Marine Station Hotel.
- Repairs are carried out on St. Paul's Church at Church Terrace, opposite the Royal Hotel.
- The Rev. George Digby Scott is elected Canon of Christ Church, Dublin.

The Marine Station Hotel was on the site where Katie Gallagher's / Ocean Bar pub is now. The ground floor (east) is the only surviving 'footprint' of the original hotel.

1911

- A branch of the Irish Transport and General Workers' Union is established in Bray.
- Christ Church on Church Road, Bray gets a new organ built by Conachar of Huddersfield, England.
- The Bray Public library on the corner of the Florence and Eglinton Road is opened on foot of a £2,000 grant. Mr William Burke is appointed manager.

2   February
- A great storm sweeps Ireland causing havoc to all areas.

12   February
- Cearbhall Ó Dalaigh is born at No. 85 Main Street. The future Chief Justice and President of Ireland is the second son of a fishmonger.

1912

- The new Cinema Theatre opens on the Florence Road (Smyths Toystore is now on the site).
17 February • Repair work is completed on St. Paul's Church and it is reopened.
1 July • Counties Wicklow, Dublin, Kildare and Meath are affected by a serious outbreak of 'Foot & Mouth' disease.
10 July • An explosion at the Bray Electric Works kills one man. A second man, was seriously injured. 41 year old Christopher Coats is the first person to be buried in the new graveyard extension at St Peter's, Little Bray.

1913

- Canon George Digby Scott's book 'The Stones of Bray' goes on sale.
3 June • Under the Shops Act of 1913, Wednesday is fixed as half-day closing day.
17 October • During the Dublin Lock Out of 1913, Police clash with dockers at Bray Harbour, when a coal boat for Heitons is off loaded.
November • A small company of Volunteers are formed in Bray, but they cannot undertake any large-scale engagements.

1914

- An organ and organ gallery is installed at the Church of the Most Holy Redeemer in Bray.
August • The International Hotel is leased from the Bethall family by the British Red Cross and St John's Ambulance Association and is converted into a hospital for wounded soldiers. It is named the 'Princess Patricia Hospital'.
1 August • 5,000 rifles are landed at Kilcoole by the Irish National Volunteers.
20 August • Artist and sculptor, Yann Renard Goulet is born in St. Nazaire, Brittany, France.

1915

- Desmond Fitzgerald, Father of Dr. Garrett Fitzgerald, is sentenced to six months imprisonment at Bray Courthouse for making a seditious speech urging young men to join the volunteers.
- A further diversion of railway track at Bray Head. This diversion involving the boring of a 1,100-yard-long tunnel by Naylor's of Huddersfield. The tunnel is the 3rd longest in the country.
7 July • The sinking of the S.S. Lusitania off the Old Head of Kinsale, Co. Cork. Albert A. Bestic (Jnr) is the 3rd Officer on board when sunk and survives. He will eventually live in Bray.

Construction on the new 1,100-yard long tunnel at Bray Head.

October	• After a sixty year battle using groynes, piles, sea walls and rock armour, the railway company capitulates and abandons 4.3 km of railway track north of Bray and moves the line 400 metres inland.

A view of the cliffs looking north showing part of the old railway track, the building on the cliff edge 'Swans Farm' eventually fell into the sea.

1916

	• An average of 4 collier boats per week unloading their cargo at Bray Harbour.
4 May	• Edward Daly is executed for taking part in the 1916 Rebellion. Bray Railway Station would later be given the name 'Bray Daly Station' on the 50th Anniversary of the Rising.
	• The Meath Industrial School for Girls (now St Patrick's on Vevay Road) closes as a school.
22 August	• The upper floors of the Marine Station Hotel is destroyed by fire. For 20 years the surviving fabric remained vacant, detracting immensely from the approach to the esplanade over the level crossing. The fire was due to defective construction of a chimney-flue.

1917

	• Construction on the 1,100-yard-long tunnel at Bray Head is completed. It will replace an earlier coastal route.
	• Due to food shortages because of the First World War, the People's Park is laid out in allotments to enable people to grow enough vegetables for their own needs.
	• The old Meath Industrial School for Girls becomes the Duke of Connaught's Hospital – for fitting artificial limbs.
	• Charles Putland's old residence, Bray Head House (Presentation College), is purchased by David Frame.
1 April	• The first meeting of the Bray & District Trade Union at the Town Hall.

1918

	• Bray Opera Company founded.
	• The Duke of Connaught's Hospital on the Vevay Road closes as the war ends, and is purchased by the Governors of the Royal Drummond Institution, Dublin.
15 April	• St. Cronan's Boys National School gets a new pupil, Cearbhall O'Dalaigh - he would later become Irish President.
October	• Bray is struck by the 'Spanish flu' (influenza epidemic) - Ravenswell school is converted to a hospital by the nuns.

| 10 | October | • The S.S. Leinster is sunk by German torpedoes 4 miles east of the Kish Lighthouse. 339 people perished. |
| 11 | October | • The Gaiety Picture House on Florence Road is gutted by fire and destroyed. |

1919

• St Gerard's Preparatory School is founded by John James at 'Thornhill'.
• Bray is struck by another influenza epidemic - seven deaths are reported in one day.
• Billy Power's film "Rosaleen Dhu" is premiered at McDermott's Cinema (old Turkish Baths), Bray.
• The Princess Patricia Hospital (International Hotel) is closed and Frank Bethell resumes possession and re-opens the building as a hotel again.
• The War Memorial is erected opposite the International Hotel on the Quinsborough Road, Bray.

One of the wards at the Princess Patricia Hospital, which closed as a hospital in 1919.

1920

• A Curfew is put into operation throughout the winter; any person found outdoors after 10 p.m. without a pass was liable to be shot or arrested. One man standing by his door near the Town Hall is shot dead by the Black and Tans.
• The old Meath Industrial School for Girls, or later the Duke of Connaught's Hospital, opens as the Royal Drummond Institution for orphan daughters of British ex-servicemen.
• The Presentation Brothers purchase Bray Head House, which was once the home of the Putland family, and open a primary and secondary school – it will become the Presentation Collage.
• Drapers and outfitters Tansey & Company are established on Quinsborough Road, Bray.

ACKNOWLEDGEMENTS

We would like to thank the following for their help in producing this book: Henry Cairns, Brian White, Karl Ó Broin, Billy Byrne, Brendan Flynn, Michael Kelleher, Cyril Dunne, Scott Vance, Willie Owens, Sean O' Hehir, Bray Public Library, Ballywaltrim Library, Presentation College, Loreto Convent, St. Peter's Church (Little Bray), 'The Well' at St. Paul's Church. A big thank you also to everyone on our Facebook page, and anyone else who contributed material. A special thank you to David Givens of The Liffey Press for all his patience, help and most of all his belief in this book. Finally, thanks to all our family and friends for all their help and support. Many people have helped us put this book together, and if we have omitted anybody it was by no means intended.